Controversies in Sociology

edited by
Professor T. B. Bottomore and
Professor M. J. Mulkay

19
A Reconstruction of
Historical Materialism

Controversies in Sociology

A Reconstruction of Historical Materialism

JORGE LARRAIN

Department of Sociology,
University of Birmingham

London
ALLEN & UNWIN
Boston   Sydney

George Allen & Unwin (Publishers) Ltd,
40 Museum Street, London WC1A 1LU, UK

George Allen & Unwin (Publishers) Ltd,
Park Lane, Hemel Hempstead, Herts HP2 4TE, UK

Allen & Unwin, Inc.,
Fifty Cross Street, Winchester, Mass. 01890, USA

George Allen & Unwin Australia Pty Ltd,
8 Napier Street, North Sydney, NSW 2060, Australia

First published in 1986

British Library Cataloguing in Publication Data

Larrain, Jorge
    A reconstruction of historical materialism.—
    (Controversies in sociology; 19)
1. Historical materialism
I. Title   II. Series
335.4′119   D16.9
ISBN 0–04–301207–8
ISBN 0–04–301208–6 Pbk

Library of Congress Cataloging in Publication Data

Larrain, Jorge, 1942–
    A reconstruction of historical materialism.
    (Controversies in sociology; 19)
Bibliography: p.
Includes index.
1. Historical materialism. I. Title. II. Series.
D16.9.L339 1986   335.4′119   85–18699
ISBN 0–04–301207–8 (alk. paper)
ISBN 0–04–301208–6 (pbk.: alk. paper)

Set in 10 on 12 point Times by Grove Graphics
and printed in Great Britain by
Biddles Limited
Guildford, Surrey

Contents

Acknowledgements

I owe a special debt to Tom Bottomore, Norman Geras, Leon Pompa, Nick Lampert and Fernando Castillo for patiently reading through the manuscript and making extensive comments. I am also grateful to Gordon Smith, David Lane, Clive Harris and Julio Faundez for their useful suggestions and to June Brough and Sue Kinchin for the typing. I owe an incalculable debt to Mercedes and Carolina Larrain for their support and understanding. They have all helped me to write a better book, although I suspect the final result is less good than they would have hoped.

Introduction

Although Habermas seems to be the first author formally to propose a reconstruction of historical materialism, many others before and after him have embarked on projects which amount to a reconstruction. Yet there is no agreed conception of what reconstruction means and of how it could be carried out. Each author has his own implicit or explicit concept and justifies the need for it in a different way. However, a broad distinction can be drawn between two types of approach. On the one hand Althusser in France and Cohen in England have proposed systematic interpretations of historical materialism, which, despite enormous differences and little regard for each other, share a concern for rigorous and scientific formulations and a belief that if historical materialism has any explanatory power it is because human actions and class struggles, social change and historical development are caused and determined by structural factors which can be precisely and rigorously defined. On the other hand, Fleischer in Germany and Sartre in France have proposed a different conception of reconstruction, which insists less on scientific rigour and structurally defined causes and more on the need to reconstitute historical materialism as a theory of practice. This means that although social change and historical development are conditioned by structural factors they must be explained ultimately as the result of human practices and class struggles which are not fully preordained.

There can be little doubt about the preponderance of the first approach within the English-speaking world. Neither Fleischer, Sartre, nor even Habermas can match the vast influence which Althusser first and Cohen more recently have exercised upon Marxist studies in the Anglo-Saxon intellectual field. I do not agree with their particular reconstructions of historical materialism because, generally speaking, I conceive of reconstruction in the second sense. Yet this does not mean that I fully agree with the way in which Fleischer and Sartre have carried out their projects of reconstruction either. My objective is to intervene in this debate on the side of the theory of practice but with a rather different concept of reconstruction which, without identifying Marx and Engels with a dogmatic and orthodox Marxism, is nevertheless more sensitive to the cleavages and disjunctures which can be found in their thought and to the need to resolve them.

There are reasons why the solutions attempted within the framework of a theory of practice are necessarily less determinate than those which emphasize structural factors only. In so far as structural relations can easily be defined as synchronic arrangements of already given elements, they, and the ascribed positional interests derived from them, can be very precisely determined. In so far as the practical political activities of classes engaged in struggle are defined by diachronic episodes which are conditioned but not entirely prefigured by structural relations and imputed interests, they cannot be so precisely determined and their outcome is uncertain. Because of this it is tempting to convert structural relations and structurally defined interests – which are only necessary conditions of change – into sufficient explanatory causes and to reduce practices – which are the real causes of change – to preordained results. But one must resist this temptation. True, it can be argued that the explanatory power of class struggle is limited because, as Cohen has suggested, it does not tell us why the successful class succeeds. But one can also argue that the explanatory power of structural factors is equally restricted because they cannot guarantee that the class that should succeed will in fact succeed. The recognition of this fact is at the centre of my project of reconstruction.

This book is not intended as an introduction to historical materialism which will allow the beginner easy and systematic access to its main tenets, but it may help the uninformed reader to clarify the issues involved in them. Although my discussion does not require specialized knowledge of Marxism, it assumes general information about historical materialism and its basic definitions. The argument is developed in four chapters as follows: in Chapter 1 I justify the need for reconstructing historical materialism and critically examine various conceptions of reconstruction. Then I propose my own conception of reconstruction in connection with the identification of some tensions in four specific areas of Marx and Engels's thought. In Chapter 2 I describe the way in which the disjunctures in Marx and Engels's theory were resolved by the next generation of Marxists and how an orthodox and dogmatic version was formed. In Chapter 3 I attempt the double task of criticizing the orthodox solutions and assessing the arguments which non-Marxist critics level against historical materialism. Chapter 4 takes all the previous threads and tries to provide some elements for a reconstruction based on a theory of practice. First, the elements of a theory of practice are put forward; second, the theoretical status and the scope of historical materialism are examined; and, finally, I attempt to show how these elements can contribute to solve the tensions existent in Marx and Engels's thought in a sense different from the orthodox solutions.

It goes almost without saying that I do not claim to have found all the answers and that the full implications of my proposed reconstruction are not elaborated in detail. Still, my purpose will be achieved if the reader comes to the conclusion that the questions I have raised and the initial answers I have given point in the right direction and constitute an incentive for further elaboration and discussion.

19
A Reconstruction of
Historical Materialism

1

On Reconstruction

Any attempt to reconstruct historical materialism involves a double assumption: first, that such a theory is valuable and can still offer important contributions to both social sciences and political practice; second, that there are specific reasons why its current formulation is not satisfactory and requires an overhauling. The first assumption cannot be simply taken for granted, especially in the English-speaking world. Many critics have accused Marxism in general and historical materialism in particular of confusion, ambiguity, lack of rigour, obscurity, vagueness, contradiction, and so on (see a survey of criticisms in McMurtry, 1978, pp. 3–18). Yet even the most virulent critics of Marxism recognize its important and vast influence: 'Marxism is such an important influence in the contemporary world that there is no need to apologise for trying to understand and assess it' (Acton, 1955, p. 1).

The question then arises why such an allegedly confused and conceptually muddled theory can still be so influential in both the political and academic worlds. The situation appears as a paradox for most critics of Marxism but it should not be so even for those undogmatic Marxists who are prepared to recognize that the standards of rigour traditionally used within Marxism have not been very high. The reason for this can be found in the principle of the social determination of knowledge: a theory cannot survive purely on the basis of a supposedly immanent force provided by its internal coherence and rigorous argumentation. If coherence and rigour sufficed, scholastic metaphysics would be extremely popular today. A theory survives and exercises influence because it can be inserted in and becomes meaningful for the practice of new generations (see Kosik, 1976, pp. 77–86 and Larrain, 1983, pp. 197–203). I want to argue therefore that the continuous development and importance of Marxism is related to its significance for contemporary forms of practice.

Perry Anderson has argued that the central characteristic of Western Marxism (mainly developed in Germany, Italy and France) has been its 'structural divorce' from political practice, its separation from the working-class movement. Western Marxism is the product of the failure and defeat of working-class struggle for socialism which resulted in a displacement of Marxist theory from revolutionary political parties to universities. This separation between theory and practice affected the content of Marxism so that discussions about the economic laws of capitalism and political strategies for socialism almost disappeared and were replaced by philosophical discourse with a special emphasis on methodological and ideological problems (see Anderson, 1979a, pp. 24–48). The idea is that Western Marxism succeeds as an academic theory because it fails politically (see also Márkus, 1983, p. 101).

The main elements of Anderson's penetrating analysis are difficult to deny: the defeat of socialist movements after the Russian Revolution, the philosophical character of Western Marxism and its emigration to research centres and university departments are all facts. Yet the way in which Anderson argues his case poses serious problems for Marxist theory. Although it may not have been intended, it seems that the connection between theory and practice which is at the centre of the social determination of knowledge does not apply to the development of Marxism itself. Thus one of the main tenets of historical materialism which relates intellectual developments to forms of social practice seems to be refuted by the very development of Western Marxism.

I want to argue that it is not possible to explain the character of Western Marxism by simply emphasizing its seeming disconnection with practice. What underlies the development of Western Marxism is not the absence of a relationship between theory and practice but rather a specific form of connection with practice. True, sometimes this relation is not easily seen. In analysing German philosophy Marx was aware of such a possibility when he tried to explain 'the apparent independence of German theoreticians in relation to the middle class – the seeming contradiction between the form in which these theoreticians express the interests of the middle class and these interests themselves' (GI, p. 195). Underneath this apparent separation Marx discovers a relationship with practice which has two dimensions. On the one hand there is a direct connection between theory and the limited practice of the class it actually represents. Thus 'Kant's good will fully corresponds to the impotence, depression and wretchedness of the German burghers' (GI, p. 193). On the other hand there is a connection between theory and the successful practice of similar foreign classes which struggle under different circumstances. Thus, Kant and Hegel theorize and develop as 'pure thoughts' and 'abstract ideas' the practical achievements of the English and French bourgeoisies.

It seems to me that this is the clue to understanding the development of Western Marxism. On the one hand it is the result of the precarious practice of the working-class movement which has been unable radically to challenge the *status quo* and which has been channelled, so far, into partial and segmented conflicts which are resolved within the framework of the welfare state. Of course, this is not a revolutionary practice but it is a form of practice none the less. To this practice corresponds the interest of Western Marxism in exploring the ideological and cultural features which have allowed capitalist societies to persuade and integrate the labour movement. To this practical reality too corresponds the theoretical search of some currents for a conception of the state which does not entail the necessity of a frontal assault in order for socialism to have any chance.

On the other hand Western Marxism is related to the success of working-class revolutionary practice in Russia first, and in many Third-World countries later on. This is an aspect which Anderson underrates. The impact of the Russian Revolution exercised a powerful influence at least until the Second World War. From then onwards the decolonization process and the development of anti-imperialist struggles coupled with the impulse of radical working-class movements in China, Cuba, Angola, Chile, Mozambique, Nicaragua, etc., have provided an invaluable source of experience and new ideas for Western

Marxism. It is important to recognize that to a certain extent European Marxism today, like German philosophy in the past, continues to discuss, theorize and develop as ideas the revolutionary achievements of non-European working classes. This ongoing practical process underpins the timeliness and relevance of academic Marxism in Europe while the practical limitations of working classes challenge its creativity to develop new ideas and strategies more adequate to advanced capitalist societies. Yet at the same time these practical circumstances underlie the serious limitations of Western Marxism, its tendency to abstraction and to conceive its own theoretical development as if it was an autonomous process. In this sense it is true to say with Anderson that Western Marxism corresponds to the impotence of the European working classes. But this is so not because it has been produced in separation from their practice but because it is somehow an expression of their limited practice. This connection with practice allows us to understand why Western Marxism cannot solve theoretically the contradictions which European working classes have been unable to solve in practice.

In a recent book Anderson (1983) seems to pay more attention to this practical relationship when attempting to explain the apparent exhaustion and crisis of Latin European Marxism (French, Italian and Spanish) by the end of the 1970s. In contrast to the ascent of Marxism in English-speaking countries he finds a marked descent in Latin European societies where it had formerly thrived. Anderson no longer emphasizes so much the 'structural divorce' from practice in order to explain this crisis but rather underlines what he calls an 'extrinsic explanation' (1983, p. 56). In analysing the factors responsible for the crisis he implicitly uses the internal and external dimensions of the practical connection which I have mentioned: thus the collapse of Latin European Marxism is connected with the failures of the Chinese Cultural Revolution and Eurocommunism – two central experiences which had purported to overcome the shortcomings of the Soviet experience (Anderson, 1983, p. 76).

However, in explaining the ascent of Marxism in the English-speaking world Anderson does not provide convincing reasons of a similar character but once more goes back to factors internal to the intellectual development of this tradition. Among them he mentions as a very important element the rise of Marxist historiography, a field in which English-speaking practitioners always stood out, and the ability to withstand political isolation and adversity which is the result of 'a steadier and more tough minded historical materialism' (Anderson, 1983, p. 77). Anderson's enthusiasm about the robustness and vitality of Marxism in the English-speaking world seems to me to require some qualification. Basically, the practical limitations underlying its development are not dissimilar to those affecting Latin European Marxism, if not even worse. True, the practical constraints are experienced in a different way. Because of the present absence of mass communist parties in the English- and German-speaking zones the rise and fall of Eurocommunism affected only Latin European Marxism and the crisis was more deeply felt by it. Yet for all its shortcomings Latin European Marxism was trying to grapple with questions which had practical relevance for relatively powerful and radical working-class movements within which communist parties played a crucial role. In the English-speaking world, on the contrary, there are no radical working-class movements of the same stature and the influence of communist parties is negligible. The result is that the vitality of Marxist theory – without denying other important achievements – largely concentrates on the analysis of the past (historiography) or, more recently, on the rehabilitation of a technologically deterministic view of history. (Among the authors of the first strand are Maurice Dobb, Eric Hobsbawm, Christopher Hill, Edward Thompson, Rodney Hilton, and Eugene Genovese. Among the authors of the second strand one can mention Gerald A. Cohen, William H. Shaw and John McMurtry).

I do not want to detract from the impressive achievements of both these lines of development. But it is possible to notice that to a certain extent they have intellectually compensated for the practical shortcomings of the labour movement. On the one hand a strand among historians has reduced historical materialism to the writing of history, thus implicitly denying its theoretical status and its relevance for the analysis of present society. On the other hand the revival of deterministic conceptions of history unwittingly replicates the petrified orthodoxy of Soviet Marxism and tends to sever the close relationships which existed between historical materialism and the idea of practice. Inevitability and necessity make up for the lack of revolutionary activity (see on this Herf, 1977, p. 135). While Western Marxism may have been guilty of excessive intellectualism and methodologism, its philosophical overdevelopment never lost sight of the practical questions related to a possible transition to socialism in advanced capitalist societies. The concern with historiography and the general conception of history in English-speaking Marxism has produced brilliant and rigorous analyses but, in the process, historical materialism has been in danger of losing both its theoretical status and its connection with practice.

So historical materialism is at the crossroads. The tradition of Western Marxism which had given to it a critical character and had tried to develop it in a non-deterministic and non-economistic manner different from the Soviet orthodoxy has entered into a deep crisis. On the other hand the new vitality of Marxism in the English-speaking world has led to tendencies which underrate the theoretical status of historical materialism or resurrect the Soviet deterministic interpretation, now with the additional power of a rigorous formulation. From this situation I derive the need to reconstruct historical materialism as a theory of practice which provides the essential elements for the comprehension of history, society and the individual in their complex relationships. I agree with Fleischer's objective of reconstructing 'Marxist philosophy as a humanist-emancipatory philosophy of practice' (1973, p. 7). The precise sense and scope of such a theory will become clear, I hope, later on. For the time being I want to focus on the meaning of reconstruction.

THE MEANING OF RECONSTRUCTION

Various authors in recent years have explicitly or implicitly proposed a reconstruction of historical materialism, but by reconstruction they have understood very different things. A first set of theories understands reconstruction as the introduction of a special method of reading Marx and elucidating what he really wanted to say. These approaches start from the assumption that Marx's propositions are unsystematically worked out and loosely presented and that, consequently, some rigour should be introduced in order to apprehend their significance and coherence. Thus Althusser suggests the existence of a consistent cleavage between Marx's explicit statements and the real scientific points which are concealed. The purpose of reconstruction is then the reconstitution of Marx's hidden scientific 'problematic' by means of a 'symptomatic reading' which penetrates the surface of his formulations (Althusser and Balibar, 1975, pp. 28–32).

Other 'methodological' conceptions of reconstruction emphasize the need for a systematic clarification and reconstitution of the categorical framework of Marxism (McMurtry, 1978, p. 18) or try to eliminate the ambiguities that litter Marx's accounts by introducing the rigour and clarity of contemporary analytical philosophy (Cohen, 1978, p. ix). The point is not so much to ascertain what Marx really meant as to discover the logical requirements of his theory. Thus reconstruction means the introduction of discipline, the straightening out of Marx's ideas. Fleischer in his turn believes that most interpretations of Marxism do not give due consideration to the complexity of Marx's thought and tend categorically to advance partial and unilateral versions. Hence the main task of reconstruction is 'to contribute to extracting the Marxist concept of history from the straits of such one-sided interpretation, to rescue it from its strangeness and make it more intelligible, and to demonstrate its elasticity and "experimental" nature instead of its alleged rigidity' (Fleischer, 1973, p. 12).

Reconstruction can also mean more than a 'methodological' approach to Marx's writings and can have stronger implications. Habermas, who gave intellectual currency to the term, defines reconstruction as 'taking a theory apart and putting it back together again in a new form in order to attain more fully the goal it has set for itself' (1979, p. 95). Yet this process goes beyond the simple rearrangement of the same elements: the theory as such 'needs revision', in particular an elaboration of its normative foundations which can only be provided by a theory of communicative action (p. 97). Sartre in his turn derives the need for reconstruction from the critical idea that Marxism has become an *a priori* and dogmatic kind of knowledge which conceptualizes events before studying them and decides in advance what the truth of everything must be (1968, p. 28). So the reconstruction of historical materialism requires the integration of new disciplines into Marxism which will 'simply reinstate concrete regions of the real' (p. 65) and which will grasp the concrete determinations of human life: existentialism, psychoanalysis and empirical sociology. Yet on the other hand this incorporation must avoid the narrowness of particular 'fields': they must be shown 'as the expression of a deeper totalising movement . . . and this amounts to requiring Marxists to establish their method *a priori*' (Sartre, 1976, p. 18).

Although I accept the premiss of most 'methodological' conceptions of reconstruction that there are ambiguities in Marx's formulations and that some ideas need to be further elaborated and sometimes straightened out, it seems to me that the task of reconstructing historical materialism goes beyond the simple introduction of rigour and systematization in Marx's theory. The problem is to identify the source of ambiguities. True, some of them are due to lack of time to develop and think through certain ideas, as Cohen suggests, but the most important of them are caused by deeper reasons which, once identified, show that the introduction of logic and discipline does not suffice to put them right. Similarly, it is of course necessary to avoid the one-sided emphasis on partial aspects of Marx's thought, but for me reconstruction means more than the thorough consideration of the totality of Marx's thought and the careful weighing up of a wide range of passages against one another, as Fleischer proposes. He assumes not only that a basic coherence can always be found but also that the result is necessarily correct and balanced. These assumptions are by no means self-evident. In my view a proper concept of reconstruction must be able to question whether all the elements of the theory are coherent and whether their specific articulation is valid; it must be prepared to find cleavages which make it necessary either to alter the balance between these elements or simply to exclude proposed solutions which do not fit.

My conception of reconstruction should also accept that occasionally Marx's own version of his theoretical activity may be incongruous with the real significance of it. However, it rejects Althusser's *a priori* idea that there is a consistent disjuncture whereby Marx's contribution is systematically concealed from Marx himself. Besides, Marx's alleged hidden 'scientific problematic' is previously defined by Althusser on the basis of criteria taken from Spinoza and Bachelard and so Marxism is reconstructed by selecting only those propositions which measure up to externally conceived criteria (See Althusser, 1976, pp. 132–141, and Echeverría, 1978, p. 13). It does not make sense to try to reconstruct a particular theory by ascribing to it a preconceived notion of science taken from other theories. Neither is it sensible to go Habermas's or Sartre's way and try to fill allegedly fundamental blanks in Marx's thought with an entirely new theory of communication or the introduction of whole disciplines independently developed, such as existentialism and psychoanalysis. Heller's indictment that Habermas 'never undertakes to dissect the delicate fibres of the tissues called the *oeuvre* of Marx, nor does he attempt to understand a *cogito* called Karl Marx' (Heller, 1982, p. 22) is also applicable to Sartre. The result is that both Habermas and Sartre tend to conflate Marx with institutionalized Marxism and to substitute general unhistorical concepts for the categories of historical materialism. Thus the shift from production to communication allows Habermas to minimize the importance of materially based class conflicts and to substitute for them the idea of 'distorted communication'. Sartre in his turn seeks to establish the dialectical method *a priori*, and hence the problems of seriality, scarcity and alienation which he identifies as confronting human beings of all times seem to shift the focus away from the historically specific forms of class exploitation. In short, both reconstructions radically alter what most people would consider historical materialism to be about.

The ambiguities which my concept of reconstruction is concerned with and which are at the origin of one-sided and dogmatic interpretations of Marxism stem, I think, from some tensions in Marx's work which derive from difficulties inherent in the very complex task Marx set himself. Three main problems are worth mentioning in this respect. First, the enormous scope of Marx's objective, which is to provide a rigorous account of the real premises which allow a proper understanding of society and history, poses the problem as to whether the concrete analyses of specific modes of production can be articulated with more general principles about their historical succession, whether the variability of particular historical cases is compatible with a unified vision of historical totality. Second, there is the problem of taking elements of different theoretical origins and from different disciplines and trying to integrate them in a superior theory. In short, I mean on the one hand the integration of materialist philosophical elements taken from seventeenth-century British philosophers and the eighteenth-century French Enlightenment with a theory of practice and consciousness which establishes the active side of the subject and whose main elements had been provided by German idealism; on the other hand the integration of such a philosophical synthesis with the empirical data provided by historical and economic analyses. Third, Marx's objective of understanding society and history is held with a view to exploring the possibilities of liberation for humankind, that is to say, he wants to develop a theory which is not only endowed 'with the precision of natural science' (Preface, CCPE, MESW, p. 182), but is also 'in its essence critical and revolutionary' (Afterword, K, Vol. 1, p. 29). Marx's attempt to construct a scientific and revolutionary theory poses the problem of reconciling general scientific laws with particular political practices and of integrating the rigorous analysis of reality as it is with the critique of its alienated and contradictory character.

The tensions in Marx's thought arise because the balance struck between these contributory factors and the emphases laid in particular contexts of Marx's work are not always the same and hence alternative explanatory approaches to the same problems can be seen to exist. Thus it is possible to find an accent on scientific laws at certain points which is superseded by an emphasis on political practices at others; sometimes Marx underlines traditional materialist premises to criticize idealism but at other times he stresses idealist premises to criticize the old materialism; occasionally the influence of the Hegelian conception of historical totality and dialectic is predominant whereas at other junctures the specificity of irreducible historical movements is highlighted. By reconstruction of historical materialism I understand the identification and resolution of these tensions in Marx's work, not in the sense of trying to smooth over manifest contradictions or trying artificially to integrate opposite approaches but in the sense of redressing the balance of some one-sided propositions and, mainly, making clear choices between alternative explanatory possibilities.

The resolution of tensions entails neither an attempt exclusively to ascertain what Marx really meant – what Marx really meant is not always clear and can also be inadequate – nor a fundamental and systematic revision of his tenets. It entails striking new balances, with the same elements, some of which are implicitly present in Marx's works and some of which are only suggested by the general logic of his thought. It also entails changing some emphases and excluding explanatory elements which do not fit. True, Cohen and McMurtry too want to go beyond what Marx meant or said to reach the logic of the system and to make sense of the theory. But their concern has more to do with making Marx's theory unequivocal than with having a better and sounder theory. This is why Cohen can separate his defence of Marx from the need to adjust his thinking to that of Marx: the defence required that every contention was 'both plausibly attributable to Marx and plausible in its own right', but once this is done Cohen develops doubts about the soundness of the theory he has defended (1983a, p. 125, and 1983b, p. 227). My concept of reconstruction, on the contrary, is not so much concerned with making historical materialism formally plausible as with substantively resolving the tensions in Marx's work so that it becomes a more adequate theory.

The integration of different theoretical strands in Marx's thought is widely recognized but quite often not enough weight is given to the fact that it is the source of tensions and ambiguities. Alfred Schmidt has penetratingly analysed the way in which such integration was achieved at the philosophical level, and has convincingly opposed unilateral interpretations of Marx's philosophical thought (1971). Yet despite his genuinely critical approach it seems to me that he, like Fleischer, underplays the tensions that emerge from such an enterprise and seeks resolutions of them which are too easily attributed to Marx himself. At the opposite extreme Korsch recognizes the existence of tensions in Marx's thought only to dismiss all attempts at resolving them. He distinguishes an 'objective formula' based on the 1859 'Preface' whereby the historical process is conceived as the development of the productive forces from a 'subjective formula' based on the Manifesto whereby history is conceived in terms of class struggle. According to him these formulae 'are two independent forms of Marxian thought, equally original and not derived one from the other' (Korsch, 1938, pp. 187 and 229). Korsch rightly believes that it is no good trying to smooth over such apparent contradiction, but he fails to see the need to resolve the tension in one way or another. Korsch's position is all the more paradoxical because in the same context he criticizes two deviations of Marxism: 'economism', for one-sidedly reducing all relations to material production; and 'sociologism', for unilaterally supplanting the importance of relations of production by 'interactions' (p. 218). But he does not analyse their origin, which is obviously connected, at least partially, with the tension he has previously identified. By refusing to resolve that tension Korsch deprives himself of the very basis on which he can expect to contribute to eliminating the deviations he has outlined.

THE TENSIONS IN MARX AND ENGELS'S THOUGHT

The idea of reconstructing historical materialism therefore entails both the recognition of some tensions in Marx's work and the willingness to resolve them. It is therefore necessary to start by identifying these tensions. It seems to me that there are four main areas which are the source of important tensions in Marx's thought: the conception of dialectic, the analysis of consciousness, the mechanism of social change and the conception of history. Let us briefly analyse each of them. In so far as the concept of dialectic is concerned it is well known that Engels's late writings introduced the idea of an independent dialectic of nature and were also concerned with establishing the universal laws of dialectic (see AD and DON). These two features have been widely contested and constitute the main source of the idea that Marx and Engels did not always have the same perspective and that Engels definitely went beyond a truly Marxian concept of dialectic which cannot do without human practice (see Schmidt, 1971; Fleischer, 1973 and Carver, 1983). This is not the moment to discuss the content of these issues, but it is necessary to affirm that the problem is more complex than the simple opposition between Marx's supposedly correct view of dialectic and Engels's alleged extrapolation and distortion of it. Although it is true that Engels elaborated his ideas on dialectic very much on his own, he was in permanent correspondence with Marx, who not only knew but also approved of his efforts (see Hoffman, 1975, pp. 15–70; and Gerratana, 1975, Vol. 1, pp. 147–184).

Contrary to Carver's idea that 'Marx never endorsed the materialist dialectics . . . that Engels was pursuing' (Carver, 1983, p. 134), a careful survey of Marx's own writings shows that a problem with the conception of dialectic is present in Marx himself. For a start he too had the idea of formally defining dialectic. In a letter to Engels Marx says: 'if there should ever be time for such a work again, I should very much like to make accessible to the ordinary human intelligence – in two or three printer's sheets – what is *rational* in the method which Hegel discovered but at the same time enveloped in mysticism' (14 January 1858, MESC, p. 93). The fact that Marx never did this may not be a matter of great regret for those who hold a sound conception of dialectic, but the fact that Marx wanted to do it shows that a synthesis able to codify the main laws of dialectics in the abstract was not totally foreign to his thought. Even more, Marx did not shrink from referring to specific dialectical laws in a context which suggests the possibility of a dialectic of nature and he specifically compared contradictions in commodity relations with contradictions in the movement of physical bodies:

> you will also see from the conclusion of my chapter III, where the transformation of the handicraft-master into a capitalist – as a result of merely quantitative changes – is touched upon, *that in that text* I quote Hegel's discovery regarding the

law that merely quantitative changes turn into qualitative changes and state that it holds good alike in history and natural science. (Letter to Engels, 22 June 1867, MESC, p. 177)

We saw in a former chapter that the exchange of commodities implies contradictory and mutually exclusive conditions. The differentiation of commodities into commodities and money does not sweep away these inconsistencies, but develops a *modus vivendi*, a form in which they can exist side by side. This is generally the way in which real contradictions are reconciled. For instance, it is a contradiction to depict one body as constantly falling towards another, and as, at the same time, constantly flying away from it. The ellipse is a form of motion which, while allowing this contradiction to go on, at the same time reconciles it. (K, Vol. 1, p. 106)

But most significant of all is a passage from *Capital* where Marx compares his dialectical method with Hegel's and concludes that it is its direct opposite. Whilst for Hegel the Idea becomes an independent subject that creates the external world, 'with me, on the contrary, the ideal is nothing else than the material world reflected by the human mind, and translated into forms of thought'. From this Marx derives the idea that with Hegel dialectic is standing on its head: 'it must be turned right side up again, if you would discover the rational kernel within the mystical shell' (Afterword, K, Vol. 1, p. 29). Marx's description of his conception of dialectic as a simple inversion of Hegel's conception suggests two things: first, that, although matter replaces spirit, dialectic is still an objective process whereby an ontological substratum evolves separate from human practice; second, that the scope of dialectic continues to be the same, that is to say, it is the universal principle for explaining the world.

All these quotations show that Engels's conception of dialectic was not incompatible with some of Marx's ideas. But on the other hand there are important elements in Marx's thought which are clearly at variance with such a conception. Marx's dislike of any abstract codification of dialectical laws which substitute universal principles for concrete analyses is shown in his critique of Lasalle. In a letter to Engels Marx states that Lasalle 'will learn to his cost that to develop a science by criticism to the point where it can be dialectically presented is an altogether different thing from applying an abstract ready-made system of logic to vague notions of a system of this kind' (1 February 1858, MESC, p. 95). When Marx asserts in *Capital* that the transition from manufacture to machinofacture involves a pasage from quantity to quality he does not derive this from the existence of a universal dialectical law but from a concrete historical analysis.

There is also clear evidence that Marx was not interested in dialectic as a universal explanatory principle of all things and movements. The existence of contradictions is not for Marx the result of a metaphysical principle inherent in all beings but the social result of specific transient historical conditions which can be practically altered. Thus he affirms that

> the very moment civilisation begins, production begins to be founded on the antagonism of orders, estates, classes, and finally on the antagonism of accumulated labour and immediate labour. No antagonism, no progress. This is the law that civilisation has followed up to our days. Till now the productive forces have been developed by virtue of this system of class antagonisms . . . In a future society in which class antagonism will have ceased in which there will no longer be any classes, use will no longer be determined by the *minimum* time of production. (PP, pp. 59 and 61).

This shows that, unlike Hegel, Marx conceives of contradiction as a historically limited condition of progress. It only emerges with civilization (it therefore excludes primitive communes) and lasts only up to the abolition of capitalism and the class system. It also shows that for Marx dialectic is not an independent and purely objective movement of the material world but is inextricably related to class antagonisms and class practices.

We have then in Marx himself two seemingly conflicting accounts of dialectic, a tension which derives from his incorporation of Hegelian elements in different contexts and with different emphases. On the one hand, some of Marx's accounts of dialectic tend to give the impression that his inversion of Hegel's dialectic does not affect the scope and the 'rational core' of it. Thus dialectic appears as a positive principle of universal application. On the other hand, some references to dialectic are clearly more restrictive and convey the idea of negativity, of a historically limited process inextricably linked with human practice and bound to come to an end. The problem for a reconstruction of historical materialism is not to try to determine which is Marx's authentic view — an impossible task. But, even if it were possible, it would be still necessary to examine critically the solutions which Marx and various other interpreters have given to this tension in order to see whether they are right, and if they are not, to try to give a new solution.

The second important source of tensions has to do with the analysis of consciousness. The principle that 'it is not consciousness that determines life, but life that determines consciousness' (GI, p. 37) or that 'it is not the consciousness of men that determines their being, but, on the contrary their social being that determines their consciousness' (Preface, CCPE, MESW, p. 181) is a vital part of historical materialism. Yet the meaning of this important principle is not always very clear. On the one hand there is a consistent tendency in Marx and Engels to analyse consciousness as a reflection of material life by following the basic idea of philosophical materialism: the material world is prior to and exists independently of the mind and therefore ideas can only reflect and represent, are the mere images of the objective world. Thus in *The German Ideology* Marx and Engels speak of 'ideological reflexes and echoes of this life-process', 'sublimates of their material life-process' and 'the ideal reflection of real collisions' (GI, pp. 36 and 287). In this text they introduce for the first time the idea that consciousness is the superstructure of a material basis (GI, p. 89), a metaphor which they will consistently use to explain the principle that consciousness is not autonomous but determined. Later, in *Capital*, Marx reaffirms that for him 'the ideal is nothing else than the material world reflected by the human mind, and translated into forms of thought' (Afterword, K, Vol. 1, p. 29). Engels in a letter to Mehring speaks of 'the reflection in thought of changed economic facts' (14 July 1893, MESC, p.

433) and in *Anti-Dühring* even describes modern socialism as 'nothing but the reflex in thought' of the conflict between productive forces and modes of production (AD, p. 317). In his *Ludwig Feuerbach* Engels reaffirms once more the materialist principle: 'we comprehend the concepts in our heads once more materialistically – as images [*Abbilder*] of real things' (LF, MESW, p. 609). The theory of reflection emphasizes the idea of consciousness being an expression of and an efflux from the material world but it does not of itself concede any active role to consciousness. On the contrary, consciousness tends to appear as a passive result which only reproduces in mind an external process which is itself constituted independently of consciousness. Yet on the other hand Marx and Engels emphasize the active side and the anticipatory character of consciousness. From the time they broke with Feuerbach they were aware that 'the chief defect of all previous materialism . . . is that things, reality, sensuousness are conceived only in the form of the *object or contemplation*, but not as *sensuous human activity, practice*, not subjectively (TOF, No. 1, GI, p. 3). This suggests that consciousness is not only an expression but also a constitutive element of reality in so far as this reality is not already given but constructed by human practice. And human practice is characterized not only by being conscious but also by the fact that, unlike animal activity, it has a goal that can be anticipated:

A spider conducts operations that resemble those of a weaver, and a bee puts to shame many an architect in the construction of her cells. But what distinguishes the worst architect from the best of the bees is this, that the architect raises his structure in imagination before he erects it in reality. At the end of every labour-process, we get a result that already existed in the imagination of the labourer at its commencement. (K, Vol. 1, p. 174)

Similarly when analysing the relationship between production and consumption Marx argues that 'consumption *ideally posits* the object of production as an internal image, as a need, as drive and as purpose. It creates the objects of production in a still subjective form' (Introduction, G, p. 92). From these quotations it is possible to deduce that consciousness does not only reflect but also helps constitute material reality by mentally anticipating the results of human practice. Hence we have once more two conflicting accounts of consciousness, a tension derived from Marx's attempt to integrate elements of philosophical materialism with the 'active side' developed by idealism. On the one hand consciousness is dealt with in the context of the base-superstructure metaphor as a passive reflection of material life. On the other hand consciousness is dealt with in the context of a theory of practice as an active and anticipatory element.

The third area of historical materialism which generates tensions is related to the explanation of the mechanisms of social change. Various authors have recognized the existence of an important disjuncture in this respect. As I have already shown, Korsch indentified it very early as the opposition between the objective formula of the 'Preface', which underlines the development of productive forces and their conflict with production relations, and the 'subjective formula' of the Manifesto, which stresses class struggle. Perry Anderson has more recently characterized it as the problem of the relationship between structure and subject (1983, p. 34), the problem of whether the primary motor of social change is the contradition between the forces and relations of production or class struggle. Miller in his turn points to the paradox that most of Marx's explicit statements seems to favour the primacy of productive forces whereas his concrete historical analyses violate the main tenets of technological determinism and stress the primacy of work relations and modes of co-operation (1981, pp. 99–100). Finally Magaline, following Althusser and Balibar, presents a clear-cut disjuncture between the young Marx up until 1859, who emphasises the dynamic role of productive forces, and the mature Marx of *Capital*, who favours the role of the relations of production and the class struggles they condition (Magaline, 1975, pp. 43–58).

However, an analysis of the terms of this tension shows a basic ambiguity: does the tension involve a lack of clarity as to which of the opposite poles within the same contradiction has primacy or does it result from an indecision about which of two different contradictions has explanatory primacy? For some authors like Magaline, the contradiction between forces and relations of production cannot be adequately distinguished from class struggle in so far as the latter is already present in the structure of relations of production. So the real tension is not between class struggle on the one hand and the contradiction between forces and relations of production on the other, but rather a tension within the latter between the primacy of the productive forces and the primacy of relations of production. For other authors the problem with such an interpretation is that it confuses the structural plane with the subjective plane of analysis. The contradiction between forces and relations of production is an objective, unintentional conflict. In Godelier's words, it is a contradiction between two structures which does not involve individuals or groups (1972, p. 79). Or, as Korsch remarks, in this formulation history is explained as an objective development and no historical 'subject' of that development is mentioned (1938, p. 186). On the contrary, class struggle involves the participation of classes and groups, their political organizations and a necessary reference to their forms of consciousness, intentions and strategies.

The possibility of defining the tension in these two different ways shows that there exists an even more basic disjuncture, namely, the explanation of social change in terms of a single class of contradiction which involves both subjective and structural aspects or the comprehension of change in terms of two different though articulated contradictions. In *The German Ideology* Marx and Engels seem sometimes to accept only one kind of contradiction which manifests itself in different forms:

> the contradiction between the productive forces and the form of intercourse . . . necessarily on each occasion burst out in a revolution, taking on at the same time various subsidiary forms, such as all-embracing collisions, collisions of various classes, contradictions of consciousness, battle of ideas, political struggle, etc. From a narrow point of view one may isolate one of these subsidiary forms and consider it as the basis of these revolutions. (GI, p. 74)

But at other times Marx and Engels seem to accept two different kinds of contradiction. Nowhere is this more apparent than in the Manifesto, where the idea that class struggle is the motor force of historical change is coupled with an explanation of the transition from feudalism to capitalism which contends that 'the feudal relations of property became no longer compatible with the already developed productive forces; they became so many fetters. They had to be burst asunder; they were burst asunder' (CM, MESW, p. 40).

Both terms of this basic tension allow in their turn further disjunctures. If one takes the idea of only one kind of contradiction it is possible to underline either the dynamic role of productive forces or the primacy of production relations, including here class struggle. The passage from *The German Ideology* quoted above gives the impression that it is the productive forces that predominate because in saying that from a narrow point of view one may isolate one of the subsidiary forms as the basis of revolution Marx adds that 'this is all the more easy as the individuals who started the revolutions had illusions about their own activity' (GI, p. 74). This seems to indicate that whatever the individuals did or thought of their actions, revolutions occurred and succeeded because of the character of productive forces. This is also expressed in Marx's letter to Annenkov where he states that 'the social history of men is always the history of their individual development, whether they are conscious of it or not. Their material relations are the basis of all their relations' (28 December 1846, MESC, p. 31).

Yet, on the other hand, if one takes a narrow material view of productive forces it seems that in his historical analyses Marx favours changes in the relations of production and class struggles as being prior to and capable of bringing about changes in the forces of production. Thus in describing the emergence of the first forms of capitalism Marx contends in *Capital* that it is the introduction of new forms of co-operation and work relations that brings about a change from handicraft trades to manufacture. The same 'narrow technical basis' of the handicraft continues to operate in manufacture (K, Vol. 1, p. 320). So the first stage of the capitalist mode of production, sometimes called by Marx 'formal capitalism' and based on manufacture, not only was not brought about by the prior expansion of productive forces but also was itself 'unable either to seize upon the production of society to its full extent, or to revolutionise that production to its very core' (ibid., p. 347). Therefore the change from manufacture to industrial capitalism proper could not be brought about by a prior expansion of productive forces either. On the contrary, new forms of class struggle appeared whereby capital was 'constantly compelled to wrestle with the insubordination of the workmen' (ibid., p. 346), and hence the second stage of capitalism came out of the conflict between 'the narrow technical basis on which manufacture rested' and the 'requirements of production that were created by manufacture itself' (p. 347).

Now if one takes the idea of two diferent kinds of contradiction, one structural and one between classes, it is also possible to underline the primacy of either of them without denying their articulation. Thus Cohen's interpretation accepts that major historical changes are brought about by class struggle but if one wants to know 'why class struggle effects this change rather than that, we must turn to the dialectic of forces and relations of production which governs class behaviour and is not explicable in terms of it, and which determines what the long-term outcome of class struggle will be' (1983a, p. 121). On the other hand it is possible to conceive of the structural contradiction as a necessary condition of change which nevertheless does not govern class behaviour nor can determine the long-term outcome of the struggle. This means that ultimately change depends on the effectivity of class struggle which the structural contradiction cannot guarantee. A mere condition like the dialectic between forces and relations of production cannot explain anything because it lacks causal effectivity. Only the agency of class struggle can causally explain change even if − as is the case − that agency is conditioned by structural factors.

Although it is not possible to find in Marx and Engels clear-cut and decisive quotations in support of either of these positions it seems to me that their writings provide suggestions in both directions. In *The German Ideology*, for instance, when they summarize their conclusions about the materialist conception of history, they start with the basic idea that 'in the development of productive forces there comes a stage when productive forces and means of intercourse are brought into being which, under the existing relations, only cause mischief and are no longer productive' – a clear, though clumsily put, reference to the major structural contradiction between forces and relations of production. Then they follow this up by adding:

> 'and connected with this a class is called forth which has to bear all the burdens of society . . . which is . . . forced into the sharpest contradiction to all other classes. . . . The conditions under which definite productive forces can be applied are the conditions of the rule of a definite class of society . . . and, therefore, every revolutionary struggle is directed against a class which till then has been in power.' (GI, p. 52)

This suggests the primacy of the structural contradiction and supports Cohen's interpretation.

Yet later on Marx and Engels describe the material conditions, both productive forces and relations, as being handed down to each generation and prescribing for it its condition of life but also being modified by the new generation, which 'shows that circumstances make men just as much as men make circumstances'. So in order to explain a revolution two material elements are necessary: 'on the the one hand the existing productive forces, on the other the formation of a revolutionary mass which revolts' (GI, p. 54). This suggests to me a rather different approach where the objective circumstances condition but are themselves modified by class practices and where the existence of a revolutionary mass which revolts is not necessarily predetermined by the existing productive forces. There seems to be a relative autonomy between these two elements which justifies Marx and Engels's open mind as to 'whether or not the revolutionary convulsion periodically recurring in history will be strong enough to overthrow the basis of everything that exists' (GI, p. 54).

It may be argued that some of the tensions I have shown in this area of social change are more apparent than real because they stem from mistaken definitions of some of the terms which constitute them. Thus for instance, in criticizing Cohen's definition of the scope of productive forces, Miller contends that 'unless Marx had an enormous capacity for inconsistency, he must have been using the phrase in a broader sense' (1981, p. 103). Thus he shows that in many passages Marx and Engels include modes of co-operation as productive forces and that if one takes this broader definition then there is no problem in accepting the primacy of the productive forces. Miller's argument against Cohen may be able to eliminate at least one of the possible tensions I have mentioned, but it only transposes the problem onto a different level: a new tension arises from possible alternative definitions of productive forces. The broad definition eliminates the narrowness of technological determinism and some contradictions in Marx's analyses but it makes it difficult to distinguish productive forces from relations of production. The restricted definition allows a more vigorous and clear-cut distinction between forces and relations of production but it reduces Marx's theory of history to a narrow technological determinism and makes some of his historical analyses inconsistent. In any case, Miller recognizes a tension even when adopting a broad concept of productive forces. On the one hand Marx's explicit statements about his theory of history propose a narrow explanatory mechanism based on the progress of productive forces (including work relations). On the other hand Marx's historical analyses in the *Grundrisse* show that change is also generated within the economic structure and that productive relations can be ultimately self-transforming (Miller, 1981, p. 144).

Finally, there is a fourth area of tensions which has to do with the conception of history. Of course, this is not an area independent from the three already discussed. Marx's conception of history is very much dependent on his views about dialectic, the role of consciousness and the contradiction between forces and relations of production. However, it can be dealt with separately in so far as the effects of the above-mentioned tensions on the conception of history are transposed into new specific tensions. On the one hand, in certain statements Marx describes historical evolution as a necessary process which imposes itself on human beings and which inexorably leads to a known end. This process is conceived in Marx's early writings as the necessary development of human nature and later, in his mature works, as a process of natural history subject to definite laws. Thus in the *Paris Manuscripts* history appears as a process of humanization which passes through a phase of alienation and which ends up with a restoration of the true essence of man:

> communism already knows itself as the reintegration or return of man into himself, the supersession of man's self-estrangement . . . *Communism* is . . . the true appropriation of the human essence through and for man; it is the complete restoration of man to himself as a *social*, i.e. human, being . . . This communism as fully developed naturalism, equals humanism . . . The entire movement of history is therefore . . . the *actual* act of creation of communism. (EPM, EW, pp. 347–8)

The conception of history as a process of humanization was abandoned by Marx very soon, but the idea of a necessary development leading to a known end subsisted in other formulations where history becomes an objective and natural process which takes place in accordance with universal laws. Thus in a preface to *Capital* Marx affirms that 'my standpoint, from which the evolution of the economic formation of society is viewed as a process of natural history, can less than any other make the individual responsible for relations whose creature he socially remains' (K, Vol. 1, p. 21). A few years later in an afterword to *Capital* he reaffirms a similar idea by approvingly quoting a description of his method written by a Russian critic:

> Marx only troubles himself about one thing: to show, by rigid scientific investigation, the necessity of successive determinate orders of social conditions . . . Marx treats the social movement as a process of natural history, governed by laws not only independent of human will, consciousness and intelligence, but rather, on the contrary, determining that will, consciousness and intelligence. (ibid., p. 27)

In so far as these texts seem to describe history as a necessary succession of social orders, they are complemented by the more detailed account in the 1859 Preface where it is stated that 'in broad outlines Asiatic, ancient, feudal, and modern bourgeois modes of production can be designated as progressive epochs in the economic formation of society' (CCPE, MESW, p. 182). History therefore appears as a unilinear and universal process where various socioeconomic stages progressively follow one another with the necessity of a natural process and inexorably lead to communism with which the 'pre-history' of human society comes to an end. Each antagonistic historical stage produces the material elements and contraditions for its own dissolution. Capitalism is the last antagonistic form of this evolution and so it 'begets, with the inexorability of a law of nature, its own negation' (K, Vol. 1, p. 715). That this process applies not only to British advanced capitalism is clear from Marx's remark that

it is not a question of the higher or lower degree of development of the social antagonisms that result from the natural laws of capitalist production. It is a question of these laws themselves, of these tendencies working with iron necessity towards inevitable results. The country that is more developed industrially only shows, to the less developed, the image of its own future. (Preface, K, Vol. 1, p. 19).

On the other hand there are a number of passages which deal with history in a context which underlines above all human practice and its capacity for modifying circumstances:

History is nothing but the succession of the separate generations each of which uses the materials, the capital funds, the productive forces handed down to it by all preceding generations, and thus, on the one hand, continues the traditional activity in completely changed circumstances and, on the other hand, modifies the old circumstances with a completely changed activity. (GI, p. 50).

Thus history does no longer appear as a teleological and close process:

History does *nothing* it 'possesses *no* immense wealth', it 'wages *no* battles.' It is *man*, real, living man who does all that, who possesses and fights; history is not, as it were, a person apart, using man as a means to achieve *its own* aims; history is *nothing but* the activity of man pursuing his aims (HF, p. 110).

The emphasis is put on the fact that men make history. True, they do not make it 'just as they please' or 'under circumstances chosen by themselves' (BRUM, p. 96), but they are not mere passive 'bearers' or 'social creatures' of objective relations either. Marx rejects a conception of history as 'a metaphysical subject of which the real human individuals are merely the bearers' (HF, p. 94). The idea that socioeconomic evolution can be treated as a process of natural history can be contrasted with Marx's statement in *Capital* that 'nature does not produce on the one side owners of money or commodities, and on the other men possessing nothing but their own labour-power. This relation has no natural basis, neither is its social basis one that is common to all historical periods' (K, Vol. 1, p. 166).

Together with this emphasis on history being practically made by men, Marx and Engels show a distrust of philosophical abstractions which provide universal schemes to which historical reality should be adapted. Of these abstractions they say that 'they can only serve to facilitate the arrangement of historical material, to indicate the sequence of its separate strata. But they by no means afford a recipe or scheme, as does philosophy for neatly trimming the epochs of history' (GI, p. 37). Forty-five years later Engels emphasizes the same point: 'the materialist method turns into its opposite if it is not taken as one's guiding principle in historical investigation but as a ready-made pattern according to which one shapes the facts of history to suit oneself' (letter to P. Ernest, 5 June 1890, MESC, pp. 390–1). This allows one to understand why Marx is incensed against a Russian critic who

insists on transforming my historical sketch of the genesis of capitalism in Western Europe into an historico-philosophic theory of the general path of development prescribed by fate to all nations, whatever the historical circumstances in which they find themselves. (letter, November 1888, MESC, p. 293)

So Marx rejects a unilinear and universal conception of history and also qualifies the sense in which he speaks of the inexorability of the process. In clarifying his theory about the genesis of capitalism to Vera Zazulich he contends that 'the "historical inevitability" of this process is *expressly* limited to the *countries of Western Europe*' (letter, 8 March 1881, MESC, p. 319). But he goes even further when considering the chances of a revolution in England: in answering Mr Hyndman, Marx asserts that his own 'party considers an English revolution not *necessary* but — according to historic precedents — *possible*' (letter, 8 December 1880, MESC, p. 313).

Marx's concrete analyses of non-European and colonial societies such as India and China also show that he does not believe that their internal processes follow the European pattern or are dynamic enough to take them out of a millennial stagnation. In the absolutely different historical context of Asiatic societies, where productive forces do not advance and where drastic political upheavals never seem to alter the economic basis, Marx praises the civilizing role of British rule, and although he is very critical of the brutality and arbitrariness of the colonizer he seems to maintain that the only chance of progress for Asiatic societies lies in capitalism being forcibly imposed on them by colonial powers (AOIC, SFE, pp. 301–7, 319–25 and 325–33). Whatever one may think of this position today, it is clearly opposed to a monolithic view of history. However, this in itself is the source of new tensions. Marx's articles on India and China suggest that colonialism can be the progressive historical agency for the development of capitalism in countries where it cannot spontaneously emerge. Yet when analysing the British rule in Ireland he takes a radically different view:

Between 1783 and 1801 all branches of Irish industry flourished. The Union, by abolishing the protective tariffs established by the Irish Parliament, destroyed all industrial life in Ireland . . . Once the Irish are independent, necessity will turn them into protectionists. (letter, 30 November 1867, MESC, pp. 184–5)

If Ireland wants to progress then the colonial rule which stifles its industry must be got rid of. Thus there are two opposite views latent in Marx concerning the expansion of capitalism by means of colonial rule.

The last two areas of tension in Marx's thought show with particular clarity the problems which stem from Marx's integration of various theoretical strands. On the one hand the influence of philosophical materialism and its emphasis on the independence and priority of nature is noticeable. Marx and Engels seem to be especially influenced by the contemporary enthusiasm for science and scientific laws; hence their description of social development in terms of a necessary process of natural history. On the other hand the Hegelian total perspective about history exercises considerable attraction. As Engels put it,

> it was the exceptional historical sense underlying Hegel's manner of reasoning which distinguished it from that of all other philosophers . . . He was the first to try to demonstrate that there is an evolution, an intrinsic coherence in history, and however strange some things in his philosophy of history may seem to us now, the grandeur of the basic conception is still admirable today. (RKM, CCPE, p. 224)

Yet all of this is combined with a theory of practice and a distrust of abstract philosophical schemes which counteract the idea of inevitable natural processes. Whereas the passages on necessary laws of development underline structural relations which fully shape individuals and their behaviour, political analyses and other passages forcefully emphasise class struggle and men's ability to change circumstances. These are among the tensions which any reconstruction of historical materialism has to resolve. But, before this, it is necessary to explore the way in which the Marxist tradition after the founders' death managed to construct an orthodox version of historical materialism which unilaterally stressed only one side of these tensions.

2
The Orthodox Interpretation

Although historical materialism is certainly the most important intellectual legacy of Marx and Engels's collaboration, Marx himself did not use this expression nor did he provide a formal definition and systematic treatment of its contents. Engels coined the terms 'materialist conception of history' (see AD, MESW, p. 316) and 'historical materialism' (see Introduction, SUS, MESW, p. 377) and even attempted a formal definition of it as

> that view of the course of history which seeks the ultimate cause and the great moving power of all important historical events in the economic development of society, in the changes in the modes of production and exchange, in the consequent division into distinct classes, and in the struggles of these classes against one another. (Introduction, SUS, MESW, pp. 382–3)

In fact Engels's *Anti-Dühring*, published as a book in 1878 with the knowledge and approval of Marx, contains the first account of historical materialism to be written after its initial formulation in *The German Ideology* and the 1859 Preface.

Although it is probably true that Engels exaggerated both Marx's support for the contents of *Anti-Dühring* and the collaborative nature of their theoretical views (see Carver, 1983, pp. 125–8 and 152), I have argued that one cannot easily dissociate Engels's ideas from at least part of Marx's thought and the influence which Engels's more scientific and naturalistic concerns exercised over Marx was recognized by Marx himself (see Gerratana, 1975, Vol. 1, p. 118). Yet the very existence of different emphases and concerns allows the possibility of different interpretations and this should be carefully considered when studying the way in which Marxism developed after the founders' death. Although it would be a travesty to blame

Engels for the construction of a Marxist orthodoxy, his late writings, particularly *Anti-Dühring*, were interpreted in a way that eventually led to the development of a rigid orthodoxy. As Gerratana has shown, *Anti-Dühring* fulfilled the need for a systematic and complete synthesis of socialism and as such it was hailed by Bernstein, Adler, Kautsky and Plekhanov (1975, Vol. 1, pp. 147–53). It did not matter that these authors went in different theoretical and political directions, they all interpreted *Anti-Dühring* as a general world view, as an encyclopaedic manual of Marxism which is separated from its critical origins. Once this is done the way is open to the dogmatic codification of principles which characterises orthodoxy.

In trying to understand how historical materialism developed into an orthodoxy one has to avoid two extremes. On the one hand it is not possible to sustain the view that orthodox Marxism is a mere distortion of the authentic thought of Marx, as Schmidt (1971) and Fleischer (1973) seem to believe. On the other hand one must reject the idea that orthodox Marxism is simply a further development of Marx's thought as Hoffman contends. In his words:

> to juxtapose Marx to Marxism, the original teachings to the developments which have come out of them, is as meaningless and futile as the attempt to separate the flow of a river from its actual source. For Marxism *is* the theory of Karl Marx as it has developed over the last hundred years of history. (Hoffman, 1975, p. 22)

Both extremes fail to recognize the existence of tensions in Marx's thought — the former praises Marx's theory as different from Soviet Marxism; the latter honours Soviet Marxism as a continuation of Marx. Hence they are unable to see that the emergence of orthodoxy is related to the existence of disjunctures in Marx's thought which allow unilateral emphases in one particular direction and that none the less one cannot reduce Marx's thought to the one-sided accents underlined by these interpreters.

In the emergence of orthodox Marxism one has to consider not only a particular interpretation of Engels's writings by the first generation of Marxists but also the fact that such an interpretation could find some support in Marx himself. Yet the construction of orthodoxy is not a simple result of intellectual options. Although I shall concentrate on the theoretical aspects of the problem and its connections with the work of Marx, it is necessary to recognize that the interpretation of Marx and Engels by the first generation of Marxists is very much dependent on the specific characteristics of the class practices within which these authors participate and struggle. Two main considerations are important in this respect. First, the circumstances that conditioned the strategy and political activities of the German SPD, the first major Marxist working-class party. For a recently created movement it was crucial to strengthen working-class organizations and so the constitution of trade unions and the expansion of their economic struggles was its priority. This emphasis on economic struggles was transposed into the belief that capitalism would almost automatically collapse by the simple unfolding of its inherent economic contradictions (see Laclau, 1977, pp. 126–7). In this context an economistic interpretation of Marx became predominant which underlined the inevitability of a process of 'natural history'. Kautsky was its main representative.

The outbreak of the First World War shattered these expectations and led to the division and final integration of the German SPD within the capitalist system. As Salvadori has pointed out, this paradoxical result was due to the fact that 'German Social Democracy was the first great workers' party that was compelled to deal, squarely and bluntly, with a capitalist system whose rapid end its theory had led it to expect, which instead exploded outwards in an imperialism that rallied wide mass support' (Salvadori, 1979, p. 19). The second important consideration has to do with the progressive evolution of the Bolshevik Party after the 1917 revolution towards a monolithic and authoritarian bureaucracy which monopolized the interpretation of Marx and Engels and which through the Comintern was even able to impose its dogmatic 'official line' on foreign parties (see Poulantzas, 1977, pp. 17–24 and 223–33). Thus to the economism of the second International an 'official' Soviet interpretation was added which fixed and codified the main tenets of historical materialism. The final stage of this process of constitution of an orthodoxy is marked by Stalin's famous pamphlet published in 1938, *Dialectical and Historical Materialism* (Stalin, 1976), which became quite influential and whose main contentions are still repeated and glossed by Soviet manuals (see Kuusinen *et al.*, 1963, and Kelle and Kovalson, 1973) and some Western writers (see Hoffman, 1975).

The main elements of the orthodox interpretation of historical materialism can be best described by looking at the four areas of tensions in Marx and Engels's thought in order to establish, first, the way in which they were dealt with by the next generations of Marxist theoreticians until the basic propositions were codified by Stalin; and, second, the manner in which those propositions have been expanded and defended thereafter. The character of these basic propositions can be summarised in four points. First, historical materialism is considered to be an extension or application of the principles of dialectical materialism to the study of society and history. Second, consciousness is a reflection of material reality because being, the material world, is prior to and exists independently of consciousness. Third, productive forces tend to develop throughout history and are the chief determining factor of changes in the economic structure and, through it, of changes in the rest of society. Fourth, history evolves through universal and necessary stages according to the progressive logic of natural-like laws which inevitably lead humankind towards the classless society. It is important to clarify, though, that not all the authors who have expounded or defended some of these basic propositions and who are discussed in this chapter necessarily agree on all the propositions or particular questions raised by them.

DIALECTICS AND DIALECTICAL MATERIALISM

Although Lenin confidently affirms that 'Marx frequently called his world outlook dialectical materialism, and Engels' *Anti-Dühring, the whole of which Marx read through in manuscript*, expounds precisely this world outlook' (1972a, p. 294), this is a term which neither Marx nor Engels actually used. In fact 'dialectical materialism' was a term coined by Plekhanov in 1894 as the most 'accurate description of the philosophy of Marx' in opposition to both the 'metaphysical materialism' of Holbach and Helvetius and the 'dialectical idealism' of Hegel (Plekhanov, 1972, p. 220, note). Yet undoubtedly Lenin has a point when he sees a connection between *Anti-Dühring* and dialectical materialism conceived as a general and distinct philosophy concerned with the dialectical laws of motion inherent in all beings. On the one hand Engels not only presents dialectics as a general principle of movement which can be *applied* to nature and history (Preface, AD, p. 15; for a definition of dialectic see AD, pp. 168–9) but also seeks to develop its application to nature because he is convinced that 'nature is the proof of dialectics' (AD, p. 33). Against Dühring's objection that there cannot be contradictions in real things he argues that this may be true as long as we consider them at rest but as soon as we consider things in motion, then contradictions appear: 'motion itself is a contradiction' (AD, p. 144).

By following this basic idea Engels then endeavours to show how dialectics operates in mechanical changes of physical elements and also in the process of organic life, chemical reactions and mathematics (See AD, pp. 161–170). Later, in his *Dialectics of Nature*, Engels further elaborates and extends these ideas with other examples about heat, electricity, friction, etc., drawn from physics, astronomy, geology, biology, and so forth. On the other hand, following Hegel, Engels seeks to establish and elaborate the general laws of dialectic which are abstracted from the history of nature and society. As he puts it,

> they can be reduced in the main to three:
> The law of the transformation of quantity into quality and vice versa;
> The law of the interpenetration of opposites;
> The law of the negation of the negation.
> All three are developed by Hegel in his idealist fashion as mere laws of *thought*.
> (DON, p. 62).

So, in laying down these laws, Engels is explicitly drawing on a

Hegelian conception of dialectic with the proviso that he needs to 'turn the thing round' so that the laws are deduced from nature and history and not foisted on them as laws of thought.

Yet the difference does not seem all that important when one realizes that for Hegel there was no appropriate distinction between history and nature on the one side and thought on the other. For him, the production of thought was simultaneously the process of production of nature and history so that, as Colleti has put it, 'the dialectic of ideas is at the same time a dialectic of matter' (1975, p. 11). It is true that in Marx one can find an explanation of dialectic as a 'simple inversion' of Hegel's dialectic (Afterword, K, Vol. 1, p. 29), but one can also find other passages in which the difference between the two conceptions is greater than a mere inversion (see Chapter 1). No such counterbalance is to be found in *Anti-Dühring* and *Dialectics of Nature* (See Carver, 1983, pp. 116–17), so it is not surprising that the generation of Marxists who took *Anti-Dühring* as the definitive account of Marxism underlined and tried to codify even further a Hegelian version of dialectic as the universal principle of all beings.

This is quite apparent in Plekhanov, who constitutes dialectics not only into a distinct philosophy of motion called dialectical materialism but also into a logic superior to formal logic. According to him the motion of matter contradicts the logical principle of identity because 'a moving body is at a particular place, and *at the same time it is not there*' (Plekhanov n.d.b., p. 90). In other words, following Engels, motion is a contradiction; but if this is so 'we seem to have found ourselves confronted with the alternative of *either* recognising the "fundamental laws" of formal logic and denying motion, *or*, on the contrary, recognising motion and denying those laws' (ibid., pp. 91–2). The solution to the riddle is to accept that just as rest is only a moment of motion formal logic is a particular instance of dialectical logic (p. 94). This position clarifies and formalizes some suggestions already found in *Anti-Dühring* which favour dialectics over formal logic in as much as it provides 'a more comprehensive view of the world' and 'the most important form of thinking for present-day natural science' (AD, pp. 36, 161–2 and 392). Apart from this Plekhanov very much emphasises the transformation of quantity into quality and the existence of leaps (interruptions in gradualness) in the evolution of both society and nature (Plekhanov, 1972, pp. 77–8 and 163; and n.d.a., pp. 35–7).

Lenin shows the same fascination with Hegel's dialectic and even affirms that 'it is impossible completely to understand Marx's *Capital*, and especially its first chapter, without having thoroughly studied and understood the *whole* of Hegel's *Logic*. Consequently, half a century later none of the Marxists understood Marx!' (Lenin, 1972b, p. 180). It does not matter therefore that Marx did not leave a specific analysis of the dialectical method because 'he did leave the *logic* of *Capital*, and this ought to be utilised to the full in this question' (Lenin, 1972b, p. 319). Lenin understands by dialectics the identity of opposites which must be recognized 'in all phenomena and processes of nature' (p. 360). Hence the dialectic of society is only a special case of dialectic in general which can also be found in mathematics, mechanics, physics, chemistry, etc. All natural sciences show dialectical motion in nature, 'the transformation of the individual into the universal, of the contingent into the necessary, transitions, modulations and the reciprocal connections of opposites' (p. 362).

With Bukharin and Stalin the development of orthodoxy receives a vital impulse because they elaborate, classify and fix the main tenets of what has been commonly called 'diamat' ever since. The first principles of this conception are concerned with the relationship between matter and mind, and are dealt with in the next section. But it is necessary to point out now that this in itself is a shift from Marx and Engels's conception in two closely connected respects. First, for the founders of Marxism the theory of consciousness was a part of historical materialism and it was dealt with in that context. Second, Marx and Engels's discussion of consciousness was not an abstract philosophical elaboration about mind and matter in general. Dialectic is the second part of this conception. But here Engels's elaborations about the dialectic of nature, and indeed some of Marx's own assertions, – provide a firmer ground for similar abstractions. So in its very birth as the orthodox philosophy of Marxism, 'diamat', as codified by Bukharin and Stalin, establishes the level at which consciousness and dialectics are discussed: not the concrete analysis of historical societies, but general abstract principles and classifications.

In so far as dialectic is concerned, Bukharin distinguishes two ways of regarding nature and society: the static point of view and the dynamic point of view. Only the latter is the 'correct' position because nothing is immutable in the world and so everything must be understood in its evolution from its origins to its destruction. This is the dialectic point of view (Bukharin, 1965, pp. 63–4). Additionally phenomena must be considered not as isolated instances but in their mutual relations. These are then the two basic principles which the dialectical method demands: *'that all phenomena be considered in their indissoluble relations; in the second place, that they be considered in their state of motion'* (Bukharin, 1965, p. 67). From them Bukharin derives methodological consequences for the study of society: each society must be considered in its own peculiar terms (p. 69); each social form must be studied in its internal process of change (p. 70); all societies must be considered in their growth and necessary disappearance (p. 70), and so on. The basis of motion is, of course, contradiction. Bukharin's understanding of Hegel in this respect reduces dialectic to a three-stage process: *thesis* (original condition of equilibrium), *antithesis* (disturbance of equilibrium), and *synthesis* (reconciling the contradiction) (p. 74), which he uses for classifying the types of relationship between society and its environment: stable equilibrium, unstable equilibrium with positive indication, and unstable equilibrium with negative indication (pp. 75–6).

Bukharin adds a few other elements about the transition of quantity into quality and the existence of sudden changes in nature and society (which had been an important concern of Plekhanov). But it is Stalin who finally lays down what Kolakowski has rightly called 'a complete Marxist catechism for a whole generation' (1978, Vol. 3, p. 97). The enormously influential pamphlet *Dialectical and Historical Materialism* is certainly not very creative in that all it contains has already been said by Plekhanov, Bukharin and Lenin, but it is systematically and pedagogically presented, the final version of orthodoxy. Besides it is the text that finally consecrates the derivative status of historical materialism:

Historical materialism is the extension of the principles of dialectical materialism to the study of social life, an application of the principles of dialectical materialism to the phenomena of the life of society, to the study of society and of its history. (Stalin, 1976, p. 835)

Stalin expounds dialectical materialism as a combination of philosophical materialism with a dialectical method. The former will be considered in the next section, as it mainly deals with the theory of consciousness. As for dialectics, Stalin argues that it is the direct opposite of metaphysics and possesses four main features. First, because nature is an integral whole 'any phenomenon can be understood and explained if considered in its inseparable connection with surrounding phenomena' (Stalin, 1976, p. 837). Second, as nature is a state of continuous movement where things are always arising, developing and disintegrating, phenomena must be considered from the point of view of motion and change (p. 838). Third, development in nature is not a gradual accumulation of quantitative changes but an accumulation of quantitative changes which abruptly passes to fundamental qualitative changes by taking 'the form of a leap from one state to another' (p. 838). Fourth, 'internal contradictions are inherent in all things and phenomena of nature, for they all have their negative and positive sides' (p. 840), and the conflict between these opposites is the substance of the process of development.

With small variations Soviet manuals repeat and comment on Stalin's version up until today. It is only in the West that one can find independent attempts to justify the dialectic of nature without reference to given or established principles of orthodoxy. French communists debate the issue in a highly abstract and rather inconclusive fashion but ultimately accept a separate philosophical treatment of dialectical laws because of the theoretical need for a philosophical definition of the contents of dialectic (See Sève, 1974; Cotten, 1977 and Jaeglé, 1977).

Hoffman in Great Britain defends the dialectic of nature by arguing that if we accept the existence of a human dialectics we are bound to accept the dialectics of nature for 'to understand human dialectics dialectically, we must understand their *genesis*.

And the genesis of man cannot be understood in terms of a nature which is only deemed capable of going round in circles' (Hoffman, 1975, p. 60); or, in other words, mechanical nature cannot produce dialectical man (p. 63); therefore 'unless matter *does* contain that "productivity and novelty which is called dialectic", then its historical development cannot be rationally explained; and if the development of matter is inexplicable, so too is the development of man' (p. 61). In short, for orthodoxy dialectic appears as a universal principle of motion inherent in all beings which can be presented as a general philosophy independently of social practices and whose application to society originates historical materialism.

CONSCIOUSNESS AS REFLECTION

We have seen how in Marx and Engels there is a tension between anticipatory consciousness and consciousness as reflection. After Marx's death many interpretations arise which, purporting to be Marxist, reduce consciousness to its economic conditions and deny it any active role. This happens so quickly that Engels himself in his last years feels obliged to confront these views and in a series of important letters tries to put the record straight. He readily acknowledges that

> Marx and I are ourselves partly to blame for the fact that the younger people sometimes lay more stress on the economic side than is due to it. We had to emphasise the main principle *vis-à-vis* our adversaries, who denied it, and we had not always the time, the place or the opportunity to give their due to the other factors involved in the interaction. (letter to J. Bloch, 21–22 September 1890, MESC, p. 396)

Engels's argument is threefold. First, that although the economic factor is determinant in the last instance, it is not the only determining one because 'once an historic element has been brought into the world by other, ultimately economic causes, it reacts, and can react on its environment and even on the causes that have given rise to it' (letter to F. Mehring, 14 July 1893, MESC, p. 435). But this is only a secondary effect (letter to

C. Schmidt, 5 August, 1890, MESC, p. 393). Second, that the ultimate supremacy of the economic factor over the sphere of consciousness 'operates within the terms laid down by the particular sphere itself' (letter to C. Schmidt, 27 October 1890, MESC, p. 401). Third, that the economic movement asserts itself because the effectivity of consciousness is diluted in an 'endless host of accidents' (letters to J. Bloch, 21–22 September 1890, and to W. Borgius, 25 January 1894, MESC, pp. 395 and 443).

It may seem paradoxical that Engels's late struggle against economic reductionism can provide at the same time some elements for the orthodox view of consciousness as a mere reflection of reality. But it seems to me that this is the case. It is not merely the fact that in these letters Engels still refers to consciousness as a reflection (see MESC pp. 400, 401 and 434), but also, and mainly, the fact that the treatment of consciousness is carried out not in the context of the theory of practice but in the context of already constituted spheres or instances which interact causally. On the one hand consciousness is given some causal effectivity but only as a given reflection of economic processes, not as anticipating and participating in the very construction of those processes. On the other hand such causal effectivity as consciousness is conceded amounts to very little because of its existence as a multitude of accidental forces which tend to cancel themselves out, thus allowing the assertion of substantial economic forces. Engels's analysis of consciousness in the context of given spheres of social life is, of course, best expressed in the base and superstructure metaphor.

The same paradoxical mixture between anti-economic reductionism and reflection theory is found in Plekhanov. Reviewing Labriola's seminal collection of essays (1970) he criticizes the theory of the economic factor as an abstraction which 'dismembers the activity of social man' (Plekhanov, 1976a, p. 15). True materialists, he argues, are 'averse to dragging in the economic factor everywhere. What is more, even to ask which factor predominates in social life seems to them pointless' (p. 9). What is needed is not a theory of separate forces which determine the movement of society but a 'synthetic

view of social life'. Law, morality and the state are determined
by economic relations but not directly and immediately. In
conclusion Plekhanov recognizes the anticipatory character of
consciousness: 'There is no historical fact that did not owe its
origin to social economics; but it is no less true to say that there
is no historical fact that was not preceded, not accompanied,
and not succeeded by a definite state of consciousness' (p. 23).

Yet on the other hand Plekhanov propounds a sequential and
rather mechanistic account of base and superstructure whereby
the prime cause of all social phenomena is the productive forces
which determine the economy and this in its turn determines
politics and so forth in an almost temporal sequence which ends
up in the most abstract forms of consciousness:

> If we wanted to express in a nutshell the view held by Marx
> and Engels with regard to the relation between the now
> celebrated '*basis*' and the no less celebrated '*superstructure*',
> we would get something like the following:
>
> 1) *the state of the productive forces*;
> 2) the *economic relations* these forces condition;
> 3) the *socio-political system* that has developed on the given
>   economic 'basis';
> 4) the *mentality of men living in society*, which is determined
>   in part directly by the economic conditions obtaining, and
>   in part by the entire socio-political system that has arisen
>   on that foundation;
> 5) the *various ideologies* that reflect the properties of that
>   mentality. (Plekhanov, n.d.a., p. 70).

It is not surprising therefore that for Plekhanov the psychology
of men reflects in general the structure of society and that '*the
psychology of society is always expedient in relation to its
economy*' (1972, p. 165). Once more the idea of reflection arises
in the context of the base-superstructure metaphor.

It is in Kautsky that the theory of consciousness takes a clear-
cut reductionist overtone. But, more than economic
reductionism, Kautsky propounds a materialistic conception
(very much based on Darwin) whereby consciousness becomes a

'weapon in the social struggle for life' (1975a, p. 134). In this sense men are no different from animals; they use consciousness to survive and adapt. So all forms of consiousness and especially moral rules are not arbitrary, they arise out of social needs (p. 118); 'each social form requires, to subsist, determined moral canons which are adapted to it' (p. 119). This means that moral norms vary and change with society. Yet this is not a mechanical process:

> As with moral canons so it is with the rest of the complicated ideological superstructure which rises upon the mode of production. It can detach itself from its base and, during a certain period, can have an independent existence. (Kautsky, 1975a, p. 123)

But this is no reason to suppose that consciousness determines social development. Following Engels, Kautsky accepts the existence of reciprocal interaction between base and superstructure and that ideological factors can favour economic development. But this can happen only while consciousness depends upon social life and corresponds to the social needs that generate it (p. 124).

This is the functionalist explanation of consciousness that Cohen (1978) has brought back into fashion: bases require superstructures and the character of the latter depends on the needs of the former. So, although moral canons can detach themselves and survive for a long time, the more economic development advances and creates new needs the stronger the contradiction between the ruling morality and the life of society's members. In the long term, morality is bound to change in order to adapt itself to the new social needs. Kautsky concludes then that

> historical materialism has brought down morality from celestial heights to the earth. We learn to know its animal origin and to see in which way its evolution in human society is conditioned by the evolution of technical development . . . Only the materialist conception of history completely overthrew the moral ideal as normative factor of social

development and teaches us to derive our social objectives exclusively from the knowledge of the given material bases. (Kautsky, 1975a, pp. 133–4)

And this is why he strongly argues against Bernstein, who believes that ideological factors, especially moral ones, have acquired in capitalism a greater capacity for independent action than before (Bernstein, 1975, p. 21). Kautsky's point is that human consciousness is today no less dependent upon the mode of social existence and that men do not set themselves problems for which they find arbitrary solutions at will (Kautsky, 1975b, p. 38).

With Lenin the development of orthodoxy receives a crucial contribution in so far as the theory of consciousness is concerned. From his very early theoretical writings Lenin held an interpretation of base and superstructure which emphasized the secondary and derivative character of the latter and the primacy of the former. This is expressed by a sharp distinction between material and ideological social relations. The former 'take shape without passing through man's consciousness' whereas the latter pass through man's consciousness before taking shape (Lenin, 1976, p. 318). It is only the material social relations that make it possible scientifically to observe regularities and recurrence in society. Ideological social relations do not allow a scientific study of society. So for the first time consciousness is explicitly excluded from the very constitution of material social relations and so the base-superstructure metaphor becomes the expression of different compartments of social life.

These early views are complemented by Lenin's defence of philosophical materialism and in particular of the theory of reflection according to which things exist outside us and are reflected as images in our consciousness (Lenin, 1972a, p. 119). As he puts it, 'matter is a philosophical category denoting the objective reality which is given to man by his sensations, and which is copied, photographed and reflected by our sensations, while existing independently of them' (p. 145). This also means that matter is 'primary' and consciousness is 'secondary' (p. 38). What is interesting in Lenin's discussion of matter and consciousness is that for the first time it is separated from historical materialism and is clearly located in the context of this new philosophical discipline called dialectical materialism which is abstract and unhistorical.

As with other aspects of orthodoxy it is Bukharin and Stalin who finally codify and fix the doctrine concerning consciousness as one of the two main subjects of dialectical materialism. Bukharin starts with the idea that first there was matter incapable of thought and then matter developed into man, who can think. So 'matter is the mother of mind; mind is not the mother of matter . . . mind comes later and we must therefore consider it the offspring, and not the parent' (Bukharin, 1965, p. 54). From this Bukharin concludes that matter exists without mind as an objective and independent being whereas mind cannot exist without matter. Society itself, being a product of nature, is founded upon material production, and without the material productive forces there cannot be social consciousness. It is 'the evolution of material production, that creates the foundation for the growth of the so-called "mental culture" . . . *the mental life of society is a function of the forces of production*' (p. 61). Of course, this does not mean that ideas have no effects but one must ask why people think in a particular way and the answer will be found in the material conditions of society.

Stalin in his turn numbers the principles of Marxist philosophical materialism in order. First, materialism maintains that 'the world is by its very nature *material*' (Stalin, 1976, p. 844). Second, it holds that 'matter, nature, being, is an objective reality existing outside and independent of our consciousness' (p. 845). As a consequence of this, matter is primary; consciousness is secondary and derivative because it is a reflection of matter. Third, materialism maintains that 'the world and its laws are fully knowable' (p. 846) and that the knowledge of them is valid and authentic. This is not true only of nature but also of society; 'hence, the science of the history of society, despite all the complexity of the phenomena of social life, can become as precise a science as, let us say, biology' (p. 849). At the same time if matter is primary and consciousness secondary it follows that the material life of society is also primary and its spiritual life is secondary and derivative. Once more it is stated that of course this does not mean that ideas are of no significance or that they do not 'reciprocally affect social being' (p. 851). Like Bukharin, Stalin takes Marx's early dictum that theory becomes a material force once it has gripped the masses, but such a theory can only emerge as a consequence of the tasks set by the development of material life.

There is very little else worth mentioning in subsequent Soviet texts, which for the most part repeat Stalin and Lenin (see for instance Kelle and Kovalson, 1973, pp. 60–64). Of more interest is Hoffman's defence of the theory of reflection. Of course he starts as any good champion of orthodoxy, by assuming the absolute theoretical coherence and the total and perfect identity of views between Marx, Engels and Lenin. In the case of the latter he shows, with some reason, that Lenin did not waver in his support for the theory in his philosophical notebooks. But beyond this he defends the theory of reflection on various grounds. First, if one does not accept the theory of reflection our relationship to the world would be unintelligible, it would be impossible to know that there is any correspondence between our mind and the external world (Hoffman, 1975, p. 73). Second, reflection does not of itself entail passivity but is an active process. Even when Lenin uses terms such as 'copying', 'photographing' and 'reflecting' he is referring to 'practical activities in human cognition' (p. 81). Third, Marx and Engels never dismissed the philosophical materialism of the Enlightenment but built on its foundations (p. 83). Fourth, and most important, the theory of reflection is crucial to understanding Marx's distinction between appearance and reality. One can only distinguish reality from appearances by accepting 'that one is a misleading *reflection* of the other' (p. 93). Fifth, 'it is only because ideas do in fact reflect the real world that human practice is possible' (p. 103). I shall critically analyse these arguments in Chapter 3.

THE PRIMACY OF PRODUCTIVE FORCES

From some of the early formulations of the 1859 Preface and of *Anti-Dühring* a tendency develops to distinguish two levels of contradictions: one which is fundamental and structural and which has nothing to do with conscious human practice; and another, determined by and derived from the former, which involves practical activities. The first level is that of the contradiction between forces and relations of production, the second is usually identified with class struggles. Referring to the former Engels affirms that

> this conflict between productive forces and modes of production is not a conflict engendered in the mind of man, like that between original sin and divine justice. It exists, in fact, objectively, outside us, independently of the will and actions even of men that have brought it on. (AD, p. 317)

The subordinate character of classes is clarified when Engels adds that socialism is an ideal reflection of the conflict between productive forces and modes of production, particularly in the minds 'of the class directly suffering under it' (ibid., p. 318). This does not mean that the two kinds of contradiction are entirely different and separate. In fact when analysing capitalism Engels derives one from the other in a mediated chain: the conflict between forces and relations of production manifests itself as an antagonism between socialized production and private appropriation and this in its turn manifests itself as the contradiction between proletariat and bourgeoisie. (p. 321)

Still the structural conflict is primary and class conflict is derived from it. What is more, within this basic conflict it is the productive forces that have the primacy, that constitute the dynamic aspect. This primacy exists even when there is no conflict with relations of production. To the question of why men enter into certain social relations Plekhanov answers that this is the result of 'the state of their productive forces' which do not depend on human will (n.d.a., p. 84). Plekhanov describes this relationship as causal: 'a certain state of the productive forces *is the cause* of the given production relations' (p. 54). Within the productive forces the means of production, especially implements of labour, play the most important role. So he can affirm that 'the whole existence of the Australian savage depends on his boomerang' (Plekhanov, 1972, p. 124).

Plekhanov proposes a functionalist explanation of political and ideological superstructures. They are what they are because they facilitate the further development of the productive forces. But eventually they become an obstacle to that development (p. 163). This is reflected in people's consciousness and leads to class struggle:

> Some members of society defend the old order: these are the people of stagnation. Others – to whom the old order is not advantageous – stand for progress; their psychology changes in the direction of *those relations of production which* in time *will replace the old economic relations, now becoming outdated.* (p. 169)

Kautsky in his turn holds that 'technical progress constitutes the basis of the entire development of humankind' (1975a, p. 81). What differentiates human beings from animals is not consciousness or tool-making, it is technical progress. Human society develops and human beings enter into multiple social relations in order to make the technical apparatus operational. Only occasionally and for short periods can social relations become obstacles to the progress of the technical apparatus. Sooner or later these obstacles are removed by internal revolutions (pp. 88–9). This account too amounts to a functionalist explanation of social relations and political superstructures. Yet Kautsky is here more cautious than any other orthodox Marxist because he does not accept that technical development is the only factor that determines the social relations of production and the political system. As he puts it:

> In several places the materialist conception of history has been interpreted as if a certain technique produced a certain mode of production and even a certain political and social form. However, as this does not happen, since we find the same tools in different social conditions, it has been said that the materialist conception of history is false and that social relations are not only determined by technique. The objection is just, but it does not correspond to the materialist

conception of history, only to its caricature which confuses technique with mode of production. (Kautsky, 1975a, p. 109)

The same technical apparatus is compatible with various modes of production and class divisions. This is so because of differences in the natural and social environment. So Kautsky's technological determinism is qualified.

Bukharin too reaffirms that 'any investigation of society, of the conditions of its growth, its forms, its content, etc., must begin with an analysis of the productive forces, or of the technical bases, of society (1965, p. 120). Productive forces are for Bukharin the result of the process of 'metabolism' between society and nature and they determine the stage attained in social evolution (p. 115). Bukharin rejects the idea that nature, population growth or race are more primary factors than the productive forces and describes relations of production as an 'outgrowth of the system of technology' (p. 142). The superstructures too are directly or indirectly (through the class structure) 'based on the stage that has been reached by the social productive forces' (p. 155). In sum, the social totality in all its elements depends on and derives from technology. Social change stems from the conflict between the forces and relations of production which determines and assumes the form of class struggle. The theoretical and historical priority of the former is emphasized: 'The evolution of the productive forces places *men* in a position of outright opposed situations, and the conflict between the productive forces and the production relations will find its expression in a conflict *between men*, between *classes*' (p. 254).

Stalin confirms Bukharin's ideas but assigns a greater role to the concept of mode of production. He starts like Bukharin by denying that geographical or demographical factors can determine the character of the social system and states that the chief force which determines the physiognomy of society is the mode of production (Stalin, 1976, p. 856). This mode of production embraces productive forces and relations of production, both of which are equally essential for production. The history of social evolution is the history of the development of the modes of production which succeed one another. Yet within the mode of production the primacy of productive forces is unequivocally affirmed. All changes and developments of production

> always begin with changes and development of the productive forces, and in the first place, with changes and development of the instruments of production. Productive forces are therefore the most mobile and revolutionary element of production. First the productive forces of society change and develop, and then, *depending* on these changes and *in conformity with them*, men's relations of production, their economic relations, change. (Stalin, 1976, p. 859)

The relations of production can retard or accelerate the development of productive forces but in the long term they must come into correspondence with the level of development of productive forces. The lack of correspondence is the basis of social revolution. Here Stalin distinguishes two situations. First, the rise of new productive forces and corresponding relations of production occurs within the old system in spontaneous form, independently of the will of men (p. 869). But, after the new productive forces have matured and the relations of production have become their fetters, a new situation arises whereby these relations and their upholders (the ruling classes) are 'removed by the conscious action of the new classes, by the forcible acts of these classes, by revolution' (p. 871).

Once more it is in the West, and especially in the Anglo-Saxon world, that the best and most original attempts to justify technological determinism have arisen. By chance the three most important examples were independently but simultaneously published in 1978 by Shaw, McMurtry and Cohen. According to Shaw productive forces are in the long run determinant of historical change. But the action of them on production relations is not automatic. It is necessary but it builds up as pressure which has to be substantial before fundamental alterations are brought about. Moreover, the precise nature and timing of a change in the relations of production is often determined by superstructural considerations – the ideological levels in which men become conscious of conflicts and fight them out. But these factors acquire their efficacy 'only because of the more fundamental pressure of the productive forces' (Shaw, 1978, p. 58). Productive forces are certainly influenced by production relations, but this does not imply that they are determined by them. For Shaw 'class analysis allows Marx to narrow the gulf between the "necessary" character of production relations and the "contingent" events of history . . . but it hardly permits full-blown scientific explanation or prediction' (pp. 71–2). So class struggle has a subordinate explanatory role and cannot be equated with the conflict between forces and relations of production which alone can account for fundamental socioeconomic realities.

McMurtry in his turn clearly and systematically summarizes the tenets of technological determinism. Productive forces 'are the material foundations of all human existence and expression' (McMurtry, 1978, p. 70). They 'raise men above the animals'; 'answer to and shape the objects of human needs' and 'actualize and extend human capacities'. They also 'set limits to, and ultimately subvert, the economic order' and 'inform the legal and political superstructure and ideology with their content'. Furthermore, they 'constitute the basic substance of all human knowledge'; progressively conquer scarcity and liberate men from the struggle for life. Productive forces reduce 'necessary labour' and are 'the moving power and ultimate determiner of human history'. 'Technology is, in a word, the Marxian Providence' (pp. 70–1). Like Shaw, McMurtry gives to class struggle a subordinate though important role. Yet he goes further than most authors in affirming that 'all class struggle for Marx is "political" or superstructural (p. 116). So both its subordination and importance are those which Marx concedes to the superstructures: they do influence the economic basis because and in as much as they are determined by it.

By far the most impressive defence of the 'traditional' 'technological' Marxism is accomplished by Cohen. He wants to uphold the explanatory primacy of productive forces, which means that '*the nature of a set of production relations is explained by the level of development of the productive forces embraced by it*' (Cohen, 1978, p. 139). This thesis he associates with the '*development* thesis', which maintains that 'the productive forces tend to develop throughout history' (p. 134). The primacy thesis entails that changes in the productive forces bring about changes in the relations of production. But the changes in the productive forces are not in the main determined by production relations. If productive forces tend to develop it is because men are rational and naturally tend to apply their intelligence in order to overcome a historical situation of scarcity (p. 152).

On the other hand, it is also true that production relations promote the development of the productive forces. The only way of reconciling this statement with the primacy thesis is by means of a functional explanation: the economic structure exists as such and has the character it has because it is functional to the development of productive forces (Cohen, 1983a, p. 119). As he puts it, 'relations obtain when and because they promote development' (Cohen, 1978, p. 165) or 'forces select structures according to their capacity to promote development' (p. 162). Cohen does not deny that 'major historical changes are brought about by class struggle' (1983a, p. 121) but he denies that the battle between classes is the fundamental explanation of social change. In fact the effectivity of class struggle is ultimately dependent on the character of productive forces (1978, pp. 148–9). So the primacy of productive forces does not dispense with human action; on the contrary it operates through the agency of human beings, thus guaranteeing that such actions cannot in the long term go against the development of productive forces. In other words, the existence of a social structure does not eliminate human practice but determines it (see Cohen, 1974, p. 92).

HISTORICAL NECESSITY

Of all the areas of tension in Marx and Engels's thought, the conception of history has provided the most significant elements for the development of orthodoxy. The influence of those passages where Marx refers to the evolution of human society as a process of natural history subjected to inexorable laws of development cannot be underestimated. It is here that orthodoxy finds the two reassuring guarantees it seems to require for its survival: first, the assurance that by discovering the laws of history it possesses the scientific key for understanding societies and their evolution; second, the guarantee that the process of history inevitably leads to communism. Yet from the very beginning there was a need to reconcile the inevitability of natural laws with human practice. Engels in his late years struggled with this problem as much as he did with the problem of the relationship between base and superstructure. Not surprisingly, he proposed very similar solutions to both, which heavily drew on Hegel. Already in *Anti-Dühring* Engels had approved of Hegel's idea that freedom is the appreciation of'necessity (AD, p. 136) but in his *Ludwig Feuerbach* and several letters on the superstructure he further elaborates on the problem.

Despite recognizing the closeness of human history to natural history Engels acknowledges an essential difference: in nature 'there are only blind, unconscious agencies' whereas in human history 'the actors are all endowed with consciousness, are men acting with deliberation or passion, working towards definite goals'. However, Engels insists that this distinction 'cannot alter the fact that the course of history is governed by inner general laws' (LF, MESW, p. 612). The solution he finds is the same as the one he proposes for reconciling the effectivity of the superstructures with the ultimately determining causality of the economy: there are so many wills and desired ends conflicting with each other that on the surface accident seems to prevail. The final results of conflicting actions rarely correspond with the intended goals. 'But where on the surface accident holds sway, there actually it is always governed by inner, hidden laws and it is only a matter of discovering these laws' (p. 612). In other words, necessity asserts itself through the accidental nature of human actions.

Plekhanov repeats the same argument almost word for word. Men follow their personal ends but the results of their actions are usually not foreseen or intended and so 'from the realm of freedom we thus pass into the realm of necessity' (Plekhanov, 1972, p. 108). A necessary process is that which occurs in conformity to certain laws. So, once these laws have been discovered, human practice acquires a new meaning because it can now consciously follow those laws. Thus necessity passes into freedom. Utopian socialists and French materialists also wanted to discover the law governing history, but they started from human nature and so became fatalists in the sense that 'the path along which mankind proceeds was in their imagination marked out beforehand' (p. 239). Marx on the contrary started at the opposite end by studying the productive action of man on external nature thus avoiding suprahistorical and immutable laws of development and asserting the variability of social relations. However, 'once the actual relations of men in the process of production are given, there fatally follow from these relations certain consequences. In this sense social movement conforms to law' (p. 239). To Stammler's critique that there is no sense in consciously trying to further a necessary process Plekhanov answers that

> human aspirations cannot but be a factor of the movement of history. But men make history in one way and not in another, in consequence of a particular necessity which we have already dealt with above. Once this necessity is given, then given too, as its effect, are those human aspirations which are an inevitable factor of social development. Men's aspirations do not exclude necessity, but are themselves determined by it. (Plekhanov, n.d.a., p. 85)

It is Kautsky who stresses with more vigour than anybody that Marx's conception of history is determinist and based on the discovery of immutable universal laws. Science deals only with necessary and natural relations and so it is the great merit of Marx and Engels to have shown that historical facts belong to the realm of natural necessity, thus elevating history to the category of science (see Kautsky, 1975b, pp. 26–7). Can society 'shorten and lessen the birth-pangs' (K, Vol. 1, p. 20) of its necessary development? Yes, says Kautsky, but only by assuming necessity. In short Kautsky cannot discover any attenuation of determinism (1975b, p. 27–8).

As Korsch has pointed out, for Kautsky human history in his totality constitutes nothing but an application of natural laws (1973, p. 36). In his work on historical materialism Kautsky explicitly wants to explore whether the development of society is closely connected with that of animal and vegetal species so that the history of humankind constitutes a particular case of the history of living beings, with its original laws, but having a coherent relationship with the general laws of animated nature. (Kautsky, 1927, Vol. 2, p. 630, taken from Korsch, 1973, p. 38).

This is why he even distinguishes two different parts of historical materialism. The first is the general philosophy of historical materialism which is concerned with general universal laws and the second contains the principles which rule history up until our days (Kautsky, 1927, Vol. 2, p. 615, in Korsch, 1973, p. 18). It does not matter if the latter principles are altered because the Marxist conception of history is based on the general laws. The obvious consequence of this position is the inevitability of the historical process. This does not entail fatalism because the future is not guaranteed by a superior force. But the future

is certain and inevitable in the sense that it is inevitable that inventors improve technique, that capitalists in their greed revolutionize the economic life . . . that it is inevitable that wage-earners aspire to shorter working hours and higher wages, that they organize themselves and struggle against the class of capitalists and the power of their state . . . That it is inevitable that they aspire to political power and the abolition of the capitalist domination. Socialism is inevitable because the class struggle and the victory of the proletariat are so too. (Kautsky, 1975a, p. 137)

For all the importance that Lenin gave to political practice and class struggles in the achievement of socialism his early theorectical writings are quite deterministic − not in the sense that the necessity of socialism can do without conscious political practice but in the sense that human acts are themselves necessitated (Lenin, 1976a, p. 334). Lenin repeats once more that social development should be treated as a process of natural history which is governed by laws that are independent of man's intentions. Rather, those laws determine human will and consciousness. Yet some of his formulations are unfortunate in that they suggest that the necessity of socialism asserts itself regardless of human will. Thus he affirms for instance that 'it is quite enough if, while proving the necessity of the present order of things, he at the same time proves the necessity of another order which must inevitably grow out of the preceding one regardless of whether men believe in it or not, whether they are conscious of it or not' (Lenin, 1976, p. 340). Apart from this Lenin introduces the motion of *social-economic formation*, which neither Plekhanov or Kautsky used in their accounts and which has become increasingly influential in recent times. Most Soviet manuals use this expression to refer to specific historical stages in the development of society which all nations must go through. Lenin simply defines it as 'the sum total of given production relations' (Lenin, 1976a, p. 320). Recently Sereni has argued that this is the key concept of historical materialism which the Second International omitted and which Lenin, following Marx, reintroduced (Sereni, 1971); but it seems to me doubtful that this notion can make a great deal of difference in the process of construction of orthodoxy (for a refutation of Sereni, see Texier, 1971).

Bukharin in his turn fully endorses Engels's solution to the problem of necessity and human will and upholds the idea of historical necessity: 'society and its evolution are as much subject to natural law as is everything else in the universe' (Bukharin, 1965, p. 46). This makes it possible for social scientists to predict the course of history, perhaps not yet with the precision required to establish the time of the appearance of phenomena but certainly with the ability to ascertain their direction (p. 49). Like Plekhanov, he defends determinism against the critique of Stammler and maintains that 'socialism will come inevitably because it is inevitable that men, definite classes of men, will stand for its realization' (p. 51). Thus social determinism must not be confused with fatalism.

Stalin briefly repeats the same ideas about scientific laws of history and the need for proletarian practice to base itself on 'the laws of development of society' (1976, p. 848). These laws determine that the history of development of society is above all 'the history of the modes of production which succeed each other in the course of centuries' (p. 858). According to this principle five types of relations of production are known to history: primitive communal, slave, feudal, capitalist and socialist (p. 862). It is noticeable that Stalin has dropped the Asiatic mode of production. As Kolakowski has pointed out, this is probably connected with the fact that such a concept makes difficult the idea of a uniform pattern of development for all mankind and also casts some doubts on the primacy of productive forces and the idea of inevitable progress (Kolakowski, 1978, Vol. 1, p. 350). Be this as it may, it is a fact that most Soviet manuals ever since have insisted on a universal and unilinear historical scheme which they combine with the Leninist notion of socioeconomic formation.

In the *Fundamentals of Marxism-Leninism*, for instance, it is affirmed that:

> All peoples travel what is basically the same path . . . The development of society proceeds through the consecutive replacement, according to definite laws, of one socio-economic formation by another. Moreover, a nation living in the conditions of a more advanced formation shows other nations their future just as the latter show that nation its past. (Kuusinen *et al.*, 1963, p. 125)

However, as many defenders of orthodoxy argue, determinism must not be confused with fatalism. The inevitability of the course of history does not preclude human participation but on the contrary, as Cohen avers, it is based upon what human beings are bound to do given their rational nature (1978, p. 147, note). This is why there is no conflict between the primacy of productive forces and the fact that 'major historical changes are brought about by class struggle' (1983a, p. 121). Contrary to fatalism which turns man into a puppet 'the dialectics of history is such that men change the circumstances under the pressure of the circumstances themselves' (Kelle and Kovalson, 1973, p. 37). Although there is 'an irreversible progression from an earlier stage to a later stage', the movement itself defines practical goals for human beings so that the 'knowledge of the laws of development becomes itself a force in that development' (Cornforth, 1977, pp. 27 and 30). Finally, Hoffman argues that determinism is not the negation of freedom but rather the basic precondition of freedom: 'without an understanding of necessity, of what is *needed*, activity is impossible, and without purposive activity, how can we be free?' (1975, p. 149). So for Hoffman freedom cannot transcend necessity; rather, the determinism of external laws must become a conscious self-determinism so that 'in absolute terms, freedom and necessity are identical' (p. 152).

We saw in Chapter 1 that connected with the conception of history there was in Marx a tension in the assessment of the consequences of colonialism for the development of backward non-European countries. This is one of the few areas in which the development of orthodoxy did not prove to be unequivocal and totally consistent throughout. At first most theoreticians followed the conclusions drawn from Marx's analyses of India and in general maintained the idea that the expansion of capitalism from European centres to backward areas was bound to increase their productive forces and eventually promote their industrial development. Although the theories of imperialism which emerged in the first two decades of the twentieth century were not particularly concerned with the analysis of the effects of imperialism on the dependent countries, most of them accepted, at least tacitly, that capitalist industrial development was an inevitable consequence. Thus, for instance, Rosa Luxemburg holds that 'the imperialist phase of capitalist accumulation which implies universal competition comprises the industrialisation and capitalist emancipation of the *hinterland* where capital formerly realised its surplus value' (Luxemburg, 1951, p. 419). Lenin in his turn argues in his theory of imperialism that

The export of capital affects and greatly accelerates the development of capitalism in those countries to which it is exported. While, therefore, the export of capital may tend to a certain extent to arrest development in the capital exporting countries, it can only do so by expanding and deepening the further development of capitalism throughout the world (Lenin, 1975, p. 76).

By taking this position Lenin was only being consistent with the analysis of the development of capitalism in Russia which he had carried out seventeen years before (1974). Lenin accepts that Russia is a backward country full of very resilient traditional structures and that the national bourgeoisie is relatively weak and dependent on foreign investment. Still, forcefully arguing against the Narodniks, he maintains that capitalism not only is historically progressive in general but is already developing rapidly in Russia. Backwardness, dependence on foreign capital and competition by more efficiently produced European industrial goods can slow down but not arrest capitalist development. So he can repeat with Marx that producers in Russia 'suffer not only from the development of capitalist production, but also from the incompleteness of that development' (Lenin, 1974, p. 607). Hence, Lenin's idea in 1916 that the imperialist export of capital can only further capitalist development in dependent countries only corroborates and generalizes his 1899 analysis of Russia.

However, as Warren has pointed out, Lenin's work on imperialism contains the seeds of the opposite view. Despite the formal declaration about the progressiveness of the results of imperialism

> the general thrust of his argument – that monopoly capitalism was parasitic, decadent, and stagnant compared with competitive capitalism – was bound to give the impression that the relationship between imperialist countries and colonies and semi-colonies was one of simple robbery . . . the inevitable result of this entire approach was that the traditional view that imperialism would industrialize the non-capitalist world was reduced to formal obeisance to the sacred texts. Imperialism came increasingly to be regarded as the *major* obstacle to industrialization in the Third World (Warren, 1980, pp. 82–3).

Still for a long time the official documents of the Third International upheld the traditional doctrine. Lenin's theses on the national and colonial question drafted during the second congress in 1920 even propounded that 'all communist parties must assist the bourgeois-democratic liberation movement in these countries' (Adler, 1983, p. 79), implicitly suggesting that the natural outcome of imperialism in backward nations was the creation of dynamic national bourgeoisies which must lead the liberation of their countries.

It is generally agreed that the sixth congress of the Third International in 1928 finally reversed this position (see Palma, 1978, p. 897; Warren, 1980, pp. 107–9; and Sutcliffe, 1972, p. 184) and explicitly asserted that imperialism was an obstacle to the development of industrialization and productive forces. Now instead of emphasizing the support for bourgeois-democratic liberation movements it is affirmed (in the context of the failed Chinese revolution) that 'the national bourgeoisie has definitively gone to the counter-revolutionary side by allying itself with feudal lords and imperialists' and in contrast with Marx's articles on India it is stated that 'the policies of British imperialism hamper India's industrial development and determine an increasing impoverishment of the peasant masses' (Agosti, 1976, Vol. 2, pp. 942–3). The assessment of the role of national bourgeoisies changed several times in subsequent congresses of the Cominterm and of the Soviet Communist Party, depending on international events and the interests of the Soviet Union. But the assessment of the consequences of imperialism for the Third World remains the same since 1928: imperialism is an obstacle to the development of productive forces and impedes the process of industrialization.

3

The Critique of
Historical Materialism

The schematic presentation of the orthodox version of historical materialism in Chapter 2 shows that its emergence is not entirely disconnected from Marx and Engels's thought in that the existence of some tensions in their writings allowed the first generations of Marxists to construct an increasingly rigid and dogmatic interpretation by unilaterally overrating some partial aspects and erecting them as untouchable principles of scientific analysis. Thus historical materialism has come to be a theory which is derived from supposedly universal laws of dialectic inherent in nature, which conceives of consciousness as a mere reflection of material life, which propounds a kind of technological determinism, and which results in a general, teleological and unilinear theory of history which sketches the necessary path of development of all nations. The partiality of such an interpretation clearly indicates that Marx and Engels's thought cannot be reduced to it. But if one wants a better theory of society and history it does not suffice − although it is necessary − to be aware that Marx and Engels's conception had other aspects too. After all, what orthodoxy does is implicitly to propose specific solutions to the tensions existent in Marx and Engels; it does not merely forget to consider some aspects of their thought. Hence, it is indispensable to criticize these solutions in order to show their inadequacy even if, as may be the case, those solutions seem to be most consistent with Marx and Engels's intentions. In this sense a critique of orthodoxy is a precondition of any reconstruction which attempts to propound different and better solutions.

Unfortunately, there exists a great deal of confusion among the critics of historical materialism about the precise subject of their critiques. Very few are able to distinguish between Marx and Engels's complex thought on the one hand and the development of a particular orthodox interpretation on the other. Thus most of the time they address their criticisms to Marxism, as a general, all-encompassing category, or, what is worse, they attribute to Marx what in effect are either rather crude simplifications taken from some manual or some particular interpretation of other authors. It is therefore necessary to bear this in mind when attempting a critique and reconstruction of historical materialism in order to avoid confusions and do justice to both Marx's thought and historical materialism. I do not start from the assumption that orthodoxy has nothing to do with the genuine development of Marx and Engels's ideas, but on the other hand I refuse simply to identify one with the other. This is an indispensable premiss of any reasonable critique of historical materialism.

THE PROBLEMS OF DIAMAT

Dialectical materialism basically develops two points: a conception of dialectics and the theory of consciousness. I start with the former. When Engels affirms that he and Marx rescue dialectics from idealism and 'apply' it to nature and history (AD, p. 15), he is implicitly taking dialectics to be a 'method' which stands on its own and which can be used in two areas of application. This separation of the 'method' from the 'object' of study or 'area' of application is at the centre of dialectical materialism. I have already pointed out that in conceiving dialectics as a separate method and trying to establish the 'laws' of such a method Engels thought that he was following Hegel except that it was necessary to 'turn the thing round' so as not to conceive such laws as pure laws of thought. I also mentioned Colletti's remark that, as Hegel did not distinguish between matter and thought, dialectical materialism ended up adopting a totally Hegelian dialectic of matter (Colletti, 1975, p. 12). Yet from another point of view diamat can be said to be profoundly anti-Hegelian and rather positivist, for Hegel did not accept the separations of method and the object of study. On the contrary, he argued that true scientific knowledge . . . demands abandonment to the very life of the object . . . It is therefore needless to apply a formal scheme to the concrete content in an external fashion . . . This nature of scientific method, which consists partly in being inseparable from the content . . . (Hegel, 1977, pp. 112 and 115)

Marx too believes that scientific method – both the method of presentation and the method of inquiry – has to follow the movement of the object: the latter has to 'analyse its different forms of development to trace out their inner connexion. Only after this work is done, can the actual movement be adequately described' (Afterword, K, Vol. 1, p. 28).

The main problem of conceiving dialectics as a separate method derived from three universal laws is its abstraction, its loss of contact with the historically concrete situation, its inability to discriminate between the substantive differences of the concrete, its reduction of the richness of life to the uniformity of abstract principles. But most of all, such a conception inevitably falls into the trap it wanted to avoid, namely, to conceive dialectical laws as pure laws of thought, as *a priori* principles which can be applied to reality. In fact if anything can be called 'dialectic' it is not a methodology but the movement of reality itself. The method is 'dialectical' only in so far as it captures and expresses the movement of the object, only in so far as being an intellectual activity it is also a part of the movement of the object. In this sense Marxist and Hegelian dialectic share the same conception of method. As Echeverría has put it, for Marx and Hegel 'method is only the form given to the theoretical activity of the internal movement of a particular content' (1978, p. 254). So dialectic is not primarily a method or separate logic of analysis – even if Marx frequently presented it as such. It is rather the specific form of movement of the reality which has to be appropriated by the theoretician.

However, the fact that Marxist and Hegelian dialectic agree on the idea of method as subordinated to the movement of the object does not mean that they should necessarily agree on their account of dialectical movement itself. Hegel's description of such movement is based on a universal concept of contradiction, which, being inherent in all beings, allows them to change and develop: 'contradiction is the very moving principle of the world: and it is ridiculous to say that contradiction is unthinkable' (Hegel, 1975, p. 174). The concept of contradiction refers to an inclusive opposition between two extremes which cannot be defined or subsist on their own without a reference to the opposite (Colletti, 1975, p. 6). Its universality for Hegel stems from the fact that it is inherent in the process of the self-alienation of consciousness which in turn is the process of creation of materiality, so that all that exists is the contradictory opposite of self-consciousness or rather self-consciousness as the opposite of itself. Starting from this notion, dialectical materialism has only to substitute the movement of matter for the movement of consciousness in order to propose a dialectic of nature independent of human society. Yet it continues to uphold contradiction as a general metaphysical principle which purports to explain the development of everything. Historical materialism is not interested in a general concept of contradiction which solely emphasizes the inclusive opposition between two material poles but focuses on antagonisms which are derived from 'human self-estrangement', from an alienated practice. Nature on its own contains either non-inclusive oppositions, real extremes which cannot be mediated (CHDS, EW, p. 155), or inclusive oppositions which do not entail human alienation. As Bhaskar has pointed out, there may be 'inclusive oppositions in nature, but not dialectical intelligibility or reason' (1983, p. 127).

A concept of contradiction which only underlines general inclusive oppositions as the source of all movement cannot express the kind of negativity historical materialism is concerned with and is bound to accept Hegel's idea that 'it is not, so to speak, a blemish, an imperfection or a defect in something if a contradiction can be pointed out in it' (Hegel, 1976, pp. 439 and 442). For Marx, on the contrary, contradiction stems from imperfection, it is the result of human beings' inability to control the social products of their practice. This is the reason why nature, considered independently of human society, does not move dialectically; it does not evolve on the basis of contradictions. This is also the reason why the scientific method of analysis of nature is not dialectical and makes no reference to the three laws established by Engels. Schmidt has elaborated this point by arguing that the dialectical laws 'have absolutely no connection with the method of natural science itself, which is oriented towards formal logic and is undialectical in the sense that it does not reflect the historical mediation of its objects' (1971, p. 55). I agree with this but it is necessary to clarify that the fact that the method of natural science is oriented towards formal logic does not mean that, *a contrario sensu*, Marxist dialectical method is not. The suggestion that Marxist dialectics entails a different kind of logic means either that formal logic does not apply in the study of society or that, to follow Plekhanov (n.d.b., pp. 91–4), formal logic is only a particular instance of superior dialectical logic which alone can understand motion.

Both alternatives are clearly mistaken. The latter, because there is no incompatibility between formal logic and movement. As Kolakowski has pointed out, to accept such naivety is to fall again into the old trap of the Eleatic philosophers who tried to prove that motion was self-contradictory (Kolakowski, 1978, Vol. 2, p. 341). The former, because there is no incompatibility between formal logic and the dialectical study of society, as Marx's analyses show on numerous occasions. Take for instance one of Marx's passages in the *Theories of Surplus-Value*, where he states that 'classical political economy occasionally contradicts itself', and then a few lines below he adds that the development of political economy 'keeps pace with the *real* development of the social contradictions and class conflicts inherent in capitalist production' (TSV, Vol. 3, pp. 500–1). The first mention of 'contradictory' clearly refers to 'logical contradictions', to unsound reasoning on the part of political economy, which Marx criticizes. The second refers to 'real contradictions' inherent in capitalist production. In the same context Marx rejects the former because they violate formal logic and recognizes the latter because they exist in reality. This can only mean that Marx's method does not claim to use a logic different from formal logic. As Echeverría has argued, Marx, 'by accepting the possibility of encountering real contradictions, is not offering their existence as an *a priori* of knowledge

. . . contradictions themselves are not an inherent aspect of his method, but a contingent aspect to be found in the object of scientific analysis' (1978, p. 251). In other words, Marx's method is dialectical not because it, in itself, contains contradictions but only because it expresses the contradictory movement of social reality (on this see also Bhaskar, 1983, p. 125).

Three important consequences derive from this. First, if social reality were not contradictory, there would not be a dialectical method of analysis. Second, as Marx identifies a primitive classless period in the history of humankind and anticipates a future communist society without contradictions, it follows that social change is not necessarily an effect of contradictions and that these contradictions are only a characteristic of a limited period of the evolution of humankind. The fact that contradictions exist in society only for a limited historical time indicates that far from being 'the root of all movement and vitality' as Hegel conceived them (1976, p. 439), − far from constituting the universal principle of reality, they are rather the result of 'inverted social relations', of the inability of human beings to control the objective social conditions which they themselves have practically produced. So, in conceiving dialectics as a universal principle of movement, dialectical materialism is more Hegelian than truly Marxist, even if some of Marx's own elaborations seem to support such a view. Given the ambiguities in some of Marx's writings on dialectic it is not surprising that critics like Acton and Popper could believe that dialectical materialism was developed by Marx by closely following Hegel (Acton, 1955, pp. 81 and 100; Popper, 1976, pp. 332–3), but this has to be rejected not only because neither Marx nor Engels created diamat as a separate philosophy but also because it is not a correct interpretation of Marxist dialectics for the reasons given above.

Third, if dialectics has to do with the movement of the object rather than with a separate method or logic, it follows that it cannot claim special privileges in order to justify vagueness, loose definitions or simply contradictory statements. Bober, for instance, has argued that one element of dialectics is the 'fluidity' of definitions (1968, p. 31) and that Engels upholds this idea in the Preface to the third volume of *Capital*, where he says that 'it is self-evident that where things and their interrelations are conceived, not as fixed, but as changing, their mental images, the ideas, are likewise subject to change and transformation; and they are not encapsulated in rigid definitions' (K, Vol. 3, pp. 13–14). Popper in his turn contends that

> dialectic is vague and elastic enough to interpret and to explain this unforeseen situation just as well as it interpreted and explained the situation which it predicted and which happened not to come true. Any development whatever will fit the dialectic scheme; the dialectician need never be afraid of any refutation by future experience. (Popper, 1976, p. 334)

But dialectics is not about vagueness or fluid concepts. Engels's quotation is ambiguous because it may refer to the historical change of ideas, which is a fact, or to the way in which things and change itself are defined, which does not warrant any lack of precision. The fact that things and their interrelations change does not justify the lack of rigorous definitions. Theory must be able to explain change without requiring a permanent flux or slippage of concepts. On the other hand dialectic is not about justifying facts or developments which cannot be really accommodated by the theory. If a theory truly accounts for the movement of reality it does not need to force the elements of reality to fit the theory. Popper's problem is somehow different, and has to do with dialectical materialism not being 'a sound basis for scientific forecasts' (p. 333). Popper believes that Marxism, as a form of historicism, is about making historical prophecies and that Marxist 'predictions' have not come true. But he misunderstands the sense in which Marxism is concerned with the future. He believes that for Marxism history is absolutely predetermined (Popper, 1973, Vol. 2, p. 86). But as we shall see in the next section this is not necessarily so. As society does not evolve as a process of natural history but on the basis of conditioned (not wholly predetermined) human practice, predictions can never be other than anticipations of what human beings, given their situation, *may* attempt and succeed or fail in accomplishing. There cannot be absolute necessity for any future event to happen. Dialectics cannot claim to predict the inevitable development of the future, but this is not the outcome of its alleged scientific failure but the result of the nature of all social science.

Lucien Sève has justified the consideration of dialectics as a separate philosophy by saying that the theoretical elaboration of dialectics is a necessity if in the concrete analysis of reality one is to apply a concept which is rigorously defined. Dialectic is therefore elevated to the category of 'philosophical science' concerned with 'the fundamental laws and categories of objective knowledge and the transformatory practice of the world' (Sève, 1974, p. 31). No one would dispute that the question of what dialectic is needs to be answered in theoretical terms. But to constitute the answer into a separate 'philosophical science' is a different and rather unnecessary proposition. Hoffman in his turn justifies the dialectics of nature by saying that a mechanical nature only capable of going round in circles cannot produce dialectical man (1975, p. 60). His argument, apart from wrongly supposing that what is not dialectical must go round in circles, assumes that human beings are dialectical in their very essence and, of course, as they are part of nature, nature itself must be dialectical. Hoffman does not realize that the discovery of a social dialectic does not necessarily entail that human society is inherently contradictory. As I have already pointed out, contradiction is only a temporary historical feature of society and the whole thrust of Marx's theory was geared to the anticipation of its definitive overcoming. Historical society has been contradictory during a certain period, but this does not mean that it is always inherently so nor does it logically require a dialectical nature. For Marx contradiction is not the normal, desirable state of society. In calling the contradictory period which comes to a close with capitalism the 'pre-history' of humankind Marx shows how little 'natural' he considers it to be.

CONSCIOUSNESS AND SUPERSTRUCTURE

The second area of problems dealt with by dialectical materialism has to do with the conception of consciousness. I have already pointed out that the elaborations of diamat in this respect constitute a shift from Marx and Engels in so far as they treated consciousness in the context of historical materialism and did not indulge in abstract considerations about mind and matter in general. In fact Marx specifically stated that to deal with the relationship between consciousness and material reality at a general, abstract level makes it impossible to understand such relationship:

> In order to examine the connection between spiritual production and material production it is above all necessary to grasp the latter itself not as a general category but in *definite historical form* . . . If material production itself is not conceived in its *specific historical* form, it is impossible to understand what is specific in the spiritual production corresponding to it and the reciprocal influence of one on the other. (TSV, Vol. 1, p. 285)

It is true that in *The Holy Family* Marx and Engels see a connection between the materialism of the French Enlightenment and socialism and communism (see HF, p. 153) and that many of the tenets of philosophical materialism seem to be upheld. For instance, in arguing against the Hegelian conception of particular real fruits as effects or manifestations of the substance 'fruit', Marx and Engels maintain that 'the apples, pears, almonds and raisins that we rediscover in the speculative world are nothing but *semblances* of apples, *semblances* of pears, *semblances* of almonds and *semblances* of raisins' (p. 70), indicating that the concept of fruit is originated in the sensuous perception of real fruits and that the idea of apple is a reflection of real apples. Furthermore, they hold that 'man has not created the matter itself' (p. 56) and they insist on the existence of a real world independent of consciousness. From these and other texts Hoffman concludes that 'it is absolutely clear that it is impossible to be a consistent materialist and yet not embrace the theory of reflection' (1975, p. 85).

However the problem is not as simple as Hoffman would make us believe. It is not only the fact that one can find other quotations in Marx and Engels that give a different impression, or that in the *Theses on Feuerbach* Marx is critical of this precise aspect of the old materialism. One must also critically examine the arguments adduced in favour of philosophical materialism in general and the theory of reflection in particular, including those which may have been advanced by Marx himself. For a start the connection between French materialism and communism suggested in *The Holy Family* is far from being elaborated within the narrow perspective of the theory of reflection. What Marx and Engels emphasize of materialism which relates to socialism is the fact that 'if man is shaped by environment, his environment must be made human' (HF, p. 154) and if man gains his experience from the empirical world, that world should be arranged in a truly human fashion. The accent is not on reflection but on the practical changing of the world, a task in which consciousness cannot be conceived as purely reflective but must anticipate a world which does not yet exist.

That human beings have not created nature and that this ultimately exists independently of consciousness no one denies. But this is hardly an argument for the theory of reflection. Marx and Engels argued again Feuerbach's contemplative conception by saying that 'the sensuous world around him is not a thing given direct from all eternity', that even 'pure natural science is provided with an aim, as with its material, only through trade and industry', and that 'for that matter, nature, the nature that preceded human history, is not by any means the nature in which Feuerbach lives' (GI, pp. 39–40). But, even if after all these provisos one upholds the priority of external nature, as Marx and Engels do, reflection does not necessarily follow. Hoffman tries to justify it by saying that the theory of reflection is the only guarantee that there is correspondence between our mind and the external world. But he has not understood that the representation of such correspondence in terms of reflection is oversimplistic because in order to account for the 'external' world the mind, and above all science, have to resort to the construction of concepts which have no specific empirical referent. This is the problem of Marx and Engels's discussion of the process of abstraction and the concept of fruit. At best such an argument is partial and seems useful only to oppose Hegel's idealism. As a description of the process of knowledge it is totally insufficient: not all concepts – and, in particular, very few scientific concepts – are arrived at by means of a process of generalization of concrete individuals such as apples and pears. One has only to think of Marx's own concepts of value, surplus-value, abstract labour, etc., to realize that they do not 'reflect' a reality directly observable.

Hence the theory of reflection not only fails to account for the anticipatory character of consciousness but also fails to explain the existence of abstract concepts which have no direct empirical referent. It is therefore surprising that Hoffman should propound as the essence of his argument that the 'distinction between reality and appearances . . . can only be based on the theory of reflection' (1975, p. 93). For a start Marx's distinction was not exactly between appearances and reality because this conveys the impression that appearances are not real, that they are pure illusions. Marx distinguished between 'appearances' and 'essential pattern' or between 'phenomenal forms' and 'inner relations', but he did not oppose appearances to reality. On the contrary he explicitly held that appearances were a part of reality:

> The final pattern of economic relations as seen on the surface, *in their real existence* and consequently in the conceptions by which the bearers and agents of these relations seek to understand them is very much different from, and indeed quite the reverse of, their inner but concealed essential pattern and the conception corresponding to it. (K, Vol. 3, p. 209, my emphasis)

Now it seems to me that Marx's distinction is not only not based on the theory of reflection, but, on the contrary is an argument against it, or at least an important limit to its validity, for although it can be said that appearances are spontaneously 'reflected' in the minds of the bearers and agents of capitalist relations, the inner relations are certainly not, and can be recognized only through abstract concepts which have no empirical referent. Of course, as Marx says, there is a 'correspondence' between the essential pattern and the scientific conception that apprehends it, but this correspondence is not a reflection because the essential pattern is by definition concealed and manifests itself only through appearances and therefore can only be grasped by means of scientific abstraction.

As I have shown in Chapter 2, the development of the theory of reflection is intertwined with the base-superstructure metaphor. I have discussed some problems of this spatial image elsewhere (Larrain, 1983, ch. 5). In the present context it is necessary to deal with some critics who have questioned the concept of determination by pointing to ideas or beliefs which have survived the end of the social conditions in which they first emerged. Thus Bober points out that the ideas of Aquinas are supposed to be a specific reflection of feudalism 'and Marxians ought to wonder why the Catholic savants of today find the teaching of the Doctor eminently acceptable seven centuries later when the economic foundations are immensely different' (Bober, 1968, p. 379). A similar argument is advanced by Kolakowski:

> the fact that some aspects of the superstructure preserve their continuity in spite of profound social changes is relevant to the validity of even this diluted version of historical materialism. Christianity, like Islam, has persisted through many social and economic systems. (Kolakowski, 1978, Vol. 1, p. 367)

It is surprising that Bober and Kolakowski should accuse Marxism of not being able to reconcile the concept of social determination with the ability of some ideas to survive for many centuries. Marx was constantly facing this problem and never succumbed to the temptation of reducing the validity of ideas to the social conditions in which they were generated. Thus he stated that 'the difficulty lies not in understanding that the Greek arts and epic are bound up with certain forms of social development. The difficulty is that they still afford us artistic pleasure and that in a certain respect they count as a norm and as an unattainable model' (Introduction, G, p. 111). He made similar remarks about the use of Roman law in bourgeois societies. Furthermore, he was very critical of those who wanted to get rid of the works of art and other fruits of civilization just because they were produced within a contradictory society in opposition to the workers (see, for instance, TSV, Vol. 3, p. 261). It can be argued that this solves nothing because, although Marx was aware of the problem and did not reduce ideas to their social background in order to dismiss them, he avoided doing so only at the cost of being inconsistent with his concept of determination. But this is true only if you conceive of determination in a mechanistic and rigorously reductionist manner as a single causative act which leads to the automatic disappearance of the effect once it has ceased to operate. This is the point at which Kolakowski introduces the catch-22 situation with which he rather unfairly condemns Marxism: 'if interpreted rigidly, it conflicts with the elementary demands of rationality; if loosely, it is a mere truism' and cannot explain anything in the course of history (Kolakowski, 1978, Vol. 1, pp. 364 and 367). Yet it has 'profoundly affected our understanding of history' and 'it makes an essential difference' for our perception of Christianity (p. 369). It is necessary to reject Kolakowski's unfair and rather facile critique not only because, as McLennan has pointed out, it is a *non sequitur* to argue that a trivial or truistic theory makes an essential difference (1981, p. 11), but also, and mainly, because a concept of determination both non-trivial and non-reductionist can be elaborated on the basis of a theory of practice the main features of which were advanced by Marx himself. Two ideas must preside over such an elaboration. First, determination has to do with human beings acquiring and producing their ideas in the process of practically reproducing their material life. Second, determination is not a single causative act but a process of continuous reanimation of ideas in the context of new practices.

Perhaps the most common criticism of the base-superstructure metaphor has to do with the alleged impossibility of adequately distinguishing between the economic structure on the one hand and the legal and ideological superstructures on the other. The argument tries to show that if you cannot properly distinguish the base from the superstructure then you cannot affirm that the former determines the latter. Thus Plamenatz argues that 'every kind of social activity involves "consciousness" ' and that therefore the contrast between social existence and consciousness is misleading because it suggests otherwise' (Plamenatz, 1971, p. 42). Heilbroner holds that ideational elements are suffused throughout the body of society and that this makes it difficult 'to draw boundaries around the material sphere' (1980, p. 84). Leff in his turn maintains that the legal and political superstructure is inseparable from the economic structure and that in general terms 'the basis-superstructure dichotomy is in reality a false model' (1961, pp. 112 and 134). Similar ideas can be found in Federn (1939, p. 101) and Acton (1955, pp. 164–5 and 167).

Cohen has replied to these objections with an argument which involves two aspects. First he shows that the distinction between base and superstructure is possible in so far as the economic structure can be defined without using legal terms. Second, he shows that the distinction between social being and consciousness is possible because social being does not involve the use of ideas in its definition. In so far as the first aspect is concerned Cohen argues that the base and the superstructure can be conceived and described as separate although they are closely related and are presented together in reality (Cohen, 1970, p. 141; 1974, p. 90; 1978, p. 235). Production relations are sometimes presented by Marx in terms of property or rights over productive forces but it is possible to excise these legal terms and replace them by the term 'power' so that instead of the right to use means of production or the right to withhold your labour power you speak now of the power to use means of production or the power to withhold your labour power. This is not a purely terminological change because 'possession of powers does not entail possession of the rights they match, nor does possession of rights entail possession of the powers matching them' (Cohen, 1978, p. 219). According to this procedure, then, the difference between a proletarian and a slave is that the former has the power to withhold his labour power whereas the latter does not.

The second aspect of the argument shows that social being is not conceived at the level of social activity but at the structural level. The economic structure specifies economic roles which are occupied by human beings. 'Social being' is equivalent to the economic role which somebody occupies, but this must be distinguished from the performance of that role. The occupancy of a role, which is conceived at the structural level, does not of itself involve any use of ideas in a causation-excluding sense. But the performance of a role may involve the use of ideas in that sense. So when Marx affirms that social being determines consciousness he is propounding a perfectly assertable proposition (Cohen, 1974, p. 91). In this way Cohen is able to conclude that, if the economic base can be defined without resorting to legal relations and if social being can be defined without resorting to the use of ideas, then the causal relations whereby the superstructure is explained by the base and consciousness is explained by social being are saved from any logical problems and can be affirmed. A different but related conclusion is that, to an important extent, relations or positions defined at the structural level causally determine social activity; the occupancy of a role determines its performance.

The first part of Cohen's argument seems unimpeachable in so far as it is concerned with the exclusion of legal relations from the definition of the economic base. However, for a traditional conception of superstructure it is not entirely clear that the substitution of 'power' for 'right' succeeds in excising other superstructural elements such as moral considerations or certain forms of consciousness from the economic structure (see for instance Pompa, 1982, p. 474). This can be shown by using Cohen's example of the distinction between the proletarian and the slave on the basis that the former has the power to withhold his labour whereas the latter does not. Cohen defines power thus: 'a man has the power to ø if and only if he is able to ø, where "able" is non-normative' (Cohen, 1978, p. 220). What does it mean that the slave is not able to withhold his labour power? Cohen is not very clear about it, but in describing and answering an objection the suggestion is made that 'the reason the slave is said to lack this power is that if he does not work he is likely to be killed, and he will certainly die' (p. 222). If this is what Cohen means, there is a problem. For slaves can physically withhold, and as a matter of fact in the past have withheld, their labour power and then faced the consequences. If is it true that fear of death is a deterrent, it is also true that this fear has in the past been overcome in Rome, Haiti, Jamaica, etc., by means of moral and ideological considerations. In any case, whether a slave chooses to rebel or not it seems that he does not lack the power to withhold his labour power in the sense of having the physical ability to do so and that whether he does it or not depends on extra-economic reasons' such as fear of death or other religious considerations.

On the basis of a similar argument Pompa concludes that the conceptual distinction between base and this aspect of the superstructure is not adequate and that unless Cohen admits 'consciousness as an element in the economic structure', which entails a serious revision, then the functional relationship between them is untenable (1982, p. 474). Pompa's argument is valid against a traditional conception of superstructure which includes the forms of social consciousness. But he does not seem to realize that Cohen's position excludes consciousness from the superstructure: 'The superstructure consists of legal, political, religious, and other non-economic *institutions*. It probably includes universities, but it does not include knowledge, for knowledge is not an institution' (Cohen, 1978, p. 45). It is true that there is in Cohen an ambiguity about the contents of the superstructure, which he never precisely defines, and that in his analyses he concentrates mostly on the legal superstructure. But at least Cohen has consistently claimed that 'the superstructure is a lot smaller than many commentators think it is. It is certainly false that every non-economic social phenomenon is superstructural: artistic creation, for example, is demonstrably not, as such, superstructural for Marx' (1983a, pp. 114–5). So, even if it is true that one cannot exclude certain forms of consciousness from the definition of the base, this does not necessarily affect the base-superstructure functional relationship.

To exclude consciousness from the superstructure does not necessarily mean that one should conceive of it as an element of the economic structure, which is the alternative Pompa suggests as a possible solution. Cohen includes within the productive forces the productively relevant parts of science but, as is well known, a crucial tenet of his position excludes the productive forces from the economic structure. In as much as Cohen conceives of superstructures as consisting of only those *institutions* which are functionally necessary to the economic base, he is bound to exclude from the base-superstructure metaphor the forms of social consciousness, knowledge, art, religious and moral beliefs, etc. If universities but not knowledge belong to the superstructure, so do churches but not religious beliefs and so do art schools but not artistic creations. Cohen is more consistent in his position than Stalin, who excluded language from the superstructure but not consciousness. But I doubt very much that Cohen can claim that on this issue he faithfully represents the views of Marx and Engels, who did not distinguish between institutions and forms of consciousness in conceiving the superstructures. This is not in itself criticizable. I have also held that 'there is no sense in characterising consciousness as a specifically separate superstructure' (Larrain, 1983, p. 178). The problem exists for Cohen only in so far as he does claim to represent and defend Marx and Engels's views.

The exclusion of consciousness from the superstructure does eliminate some problems of the base-superstructure metaphor, but it does not of itself solve the problem of how to conceive the determination of consciousness. This is the problem that the second part of Cohen's argument tries to tackle with rather less success. It is not that Cohen's answer is entirely unsuccessful. In so far as he wants to prove against Acton, Plamenatz and others that the causal relation between social being and consciousness is assertable, Cohen certainly succeeds in showing that, with his proposed structural conception of social being as the occupancy of a role, there is no conceptual difficulty in asserting such a causal relation. Thus it is perfectly true that Cohen's proposition 'if a man occupies the role of a shopkeeper he will have the ideas of a shopkeeper as a result' is assertable. As Cohen himself realizes, nevertheless, the extent to which this assertion is true is another matter (1974, p. 91). However, he believes that 'to an important extent' it is true. Unfortunately the notion that economic roles defined by specific class positions directly determine the ideas corresponding to them does not work very well in reality. It is one thing to argue that such causal relation is possible without contradiction, and quite another to be able to show that social position or occupancy directly determines ideas and through them performance.

If such an equation were true, then working-class economic roles would necessarily determine revolutionary ideas and revolutionary actions and bourgeois intellectuals could not 'cut themselves adrift' from their class to become the intellectuals of the proletariat. If one really wants to explain the ideas held by a class or social group in a particular society one can not look only to the general powers or constraints inherent in their economic roles but one must examine the specific way in which those roles are performed. Ideas are produced, selected and developed in the context of social practices. If it is true that the economic roles set limits to the performance of the role it is also true that it is this concrete performance that determines the specific character of the ideas and attitudes which are held by the occupants of those roles. One cannot assert a direct and necessary relation between certain economic roles and certain ideas; or, as Levine and Wright have suggested, structurally defined class interests cannot by themselves generate the class capacities (ideological and organizational resources) necessary for their realization (Levine and Wright, 1980, p. 58). In proposing that the occupancy of a position determines ideas and performance Cohen repeats the mistake of Lukács's definition of class consciousness as 'the appropriate and rational reaction "imputed" to a particular typical position in the process of production' (Lukács, 1971, p. 51): by focusing on the ideal, pure, most rational reaction that can be ascribed to a class position he is driven to neglect the historical concrete and practical circumstances which may or may not allow consciousness to develop.

THE CONTENT OF PRODUCTIVE FORCES

Although all authors within the orthodox perspective agree about the primacy of productive forces it is by no means clear that what they understand by productive forces is the same. The problem starts with Marx and Engels themselves because they never elaborated a rigorous distinction between forces and relations of production nor did they define their content with total precision. That the problems of scope and distinction of these two key concepts are very complicated is shown by the fact that one finds very few conceptual definitions of them, most authors restricting themselves to proposing taxonomies or catalogues of elements which are supposed to belong to each category. In the English-speaking world recent restatements and defences of the traditional conception of history as the growth of productive forces have tried to remedy this situation by introducing conceptual definitions followed by precise lists of elements which, according to them, must be included in and excluded from each concept. In general terms the conceptual definitions of productive forces are similar. Thus McMurtry maintains that 'a force of production is anything that is or can be used to make a material use-value' (McMurtry, 1978, p. 55). Cohen in his turn holds that 'to qualify as a productive force, a facility must be capable of use by a producing agent in such a way that production occurs (partly) as a result of its use, and it is someone's purpose that the facility so contribute to production' (Cohen, 1978, p. 32). Finally, Shaw avers that 'productive forces are those elements which are both basic and essential to the production process, not in the wide sense of including all activities or factors which are necessary for society to carry on production, but in the narrower sense of the simple factors of the labour process' (Shaw, 1978, p. 10).

Yet despite their similarities these definitions conceal important differences and although the three authors want to uphold traditional Marxism only one, McMurtry, comes near to doing so in a strict sense. In effect, for orthodox Marxism, productive forces include not only means of production and labour skills but also people (workers) and modes of co-operation or work relations. Stalin, for instance, in describing the development of productive forces explicitly mentions manufacture which entails the same technology and tools as handicraft production but a different mode of co-operation (Stalin, 1976, p. 862), and the same thing is reiterated in modern Soviet manuals (see Kelle and Kovalson, 1973, p. 107). That people belong to productive forces is also repeated time and again (see Stalin, 1976, p. 856; Bukharin, 1965, p. 115; Kelle and Kovalson, 1973, p. 51; Bogulavsky *et al.*, 1978, p. 333). Shaw, McMurtry and Cohen, on the contrary, explicitly exclude human beings from productive forces, but they disagree about modes of co-operation, on which they take three different positions. McMurtry's account is the nearest to the traditional orthodoxy because he distinguishes between 'technological relations', which are 'the operating connections implicit in the productive forces', and the relations of production, which are 'the proprietary connections between these productive forces and their owners' (McMurtry, 1978, p. 73).

This distinction is also upheld, although in a different context, by various branches of Althusserianism. For instance, Balibar distinguishes between property relations which belong to the social relations of production and relations of real material appropriation inherent in the productive forces (Althusser and Balibar, 1975, pp. 213–4). Harnecker proposes a similar distinction between technical relations of production and social relations of production (Harnecker, 1968, p. 28). Shaw, on the contrary, defends the view that co-operation is not a productive force, although it may expand productive efficiency as any other productive relation (Shaw, 1978, p. 24). In fact Shaw includes both 'ownership' relations and 'work' relations involved in the process of production in the concept of social relations of production (p. 31). To confuse the picture even further, Cohen in his turn proposes yet another solution, which lies in between the traditional account and Shaw's version. On the one hand work relations are recognized as relations of production, yet not as social relations of production (economic structure) but as material relations of production. On the other hand, even if work relations are material, like productive forces, 'work relations are not *themselves* productive forces' (Cohen, 1978, p. 113). This means that work relations or modes of co-operation are neither social relations of production nor productive forces.

These differences in the description of the content of productive forces may seem unimportant at first glance because what really matters to a traditional conception of Marxism is the affirmation of the pivotal dynamic role of productive forces as the motor force of history, whatever their content. To a certain extent this is true. Yet on the other hand the problem of definition has a bearing on the adequate distinction between forces and relations of production and this in its turn is a necessary condition of any argument in favour of the primacy of productive forces. As Miller has shown (1981), Marx repeatedly treats modes of co-operation as productive forces. For instance in *The German Ideology* it is stated that

> the production of life, both of one's own in labour and of fresh life in procreation, now appears as a twofold relation: on the one hand as a natural, on the other as a social relation – social in the sense that it denotes the co-operation of several individuals, no matter under what conditions, in what manner and to what end. It follows from this that a certain mode of production, or industrial stage, is always combined with a certain mode of co-operation, or social stage, and this mode of co-operation is itself a 'productive force'. (GI, p. 43)

Marx affirms here that modes of co-operation are both social and productive forces. Further on this is confirmed thus: 'the social power, i.e. the multiplied productive force, which arises through the cooperation of different individuals as it is caused by the division of labour' (GI, p. 48). Elsewhere Marx speaks of 'the general productive force arising from social combination' (G, p. 700) and in *Capital* Marx repeatedly treats co-operation as a productive force (K, Vol. 1, pp. 305–17). The number and quality of texts in this sense is such that it is indeed difficult not to agree with Miller that 'unless Marx had an enormous capacity for inconsistency' he must have included modes of co-operation in the productive forces (Miller, 1981, p. 103).

This means, first, that despite their interest in defending traditional Marxism both Cohen and Shaw have not interpreted Marx correctly on this point; and, second, that at least in so far as this problem is concerned the old Marxist orthodoxy has closely followed and correctly understood Marx. But, of course, this is no guarantee of its adequacy. However, beyond this broad agreement with Marx there are further reasons to believe that the old orthodox interpretation of this issue is better than Cohen's and Shaw's. The problem of the latter stems, it seems to me, from the distinction between social and material properties of society which Cohen explicitly proposes and Shaw implicitly adheres to. Notice that, although Shaw considers modes of co-operation as social relations of production and Cohen on the contrary conceives them as material relations of production, they are both concerned with safeguarding productive forces from any social encroachment, as if they were purely and exclusively material. Cohen defines a social property in the following terms: 'a description is social if and only if it entails an ascription to persons – specified or unspecified – of rights or powers *vis-à-vis* other men' (1978, p. 94). This is an exceedingly restrictive definition, which in fact collapses the concept of 'social' into the concept of relations of production. Such a conceptualization is arbitrary and unnecessarily reductionist. A far better definition is proposed by Marx himself, when in the above-mentioned quotation from *The German Ideology* he speaks of 'social in the sense that it denotes the co-operation of several individuals, no matter under what conditions, in what manner and to what end' (GI, p. 43).

According to this, more basic, definition, when I carry an object with you, what I do *is* social independently of whether 'I do it pursuant to an agreement, or under your authority' (Cohen, 1978, p. 95). Of course the rights or powers by virtue of which we carry the object are also social properties which determine our class position within the system of production relations. But production relations are only a part of a wider network of social relations. So if we take a more general, and in my view more adequate, definition of 'social', the so-called 'technical relations' or 'work relations' are social too in so far as they entail a plurality of human beings co-operating in the productive process even if one leaves aside their relations of effective power over the means of production and each other. It is because Shaw accepts that work relations are social that he takes them away from productive forces and locates them among the relations of production. But this move is not strictly necessary either. Why should there be a problem in conceiving both relations of production and productive forces as comprising different kinds of social relations? In fact if one excludes work relations from productive forces one risks depriving that concept of the very element which, by securing a certain combination of means of production and labour skills, determines a level of productivity. How can one conceive a certain level of productivity by looking only at the material sum of means of production and labour skills? In order to speak of a degree of productivity which grows and can be measured it is indispensable to include work relations within productive forces.

HISTORY AS THE GROWTH OF PRODUCTIVE FORCES

The various positions about the content of productive forces do not alter the fact that most authors within the orthodox tradition accept that productive forces are the fundamental motor force of change in society in as much as they tend to develop throughout history and constitute the last explanatory principle of the character of the economic structure and, through it, of the character of the superstructures. Yet it is obvious that Cohen's restrictive view of productive forces, which eliminates all social properties from them, considerably narrows the explanatory principle to purely material and technical aspects. True, Cohen is aware that 'we cannot *deduce* social relationships from a material description', but he insists that 'we can *infer* them more or less confidently, by dint of general or theoretical knowledge' (Cohen, 1978, p. 95).

Since Cohen conceives of productive forces as a purely material, explanatory principle of social elements, his account of the thesis that productive forces tend to develop and grow throughout history must necessarily exclude the determination of social aspects and, of course, of production relations, and must resort to a self-propelling, autonomous mechanism of their own: a natural tendency of rational human beings to overcome scarcity. By conceiving the development of productive forces in this way Cohen falls into the same error I demonstrated in the second section: he assumes that what is rational – and there is no doubt that it is rational for intelligent human beings to improve their situation of scarcity – is what actually occurs in historical reality. I am not saying that Cohen's equation cannot occur or even that historically one cannot discover such a trend in many societies and epochs. The problem is rather that such a direct equation pays no attention to social factors which may hinder such development. But then Cohen's theory cannot allow that, except as a temporary irregularity, because by definition social relations are supposed to be created to help promote the development of productive forces.

In theory Cohen's account is perfectly logical. The problem is that historical reality does not necessarily adapt to that logic without the mediation of specific social conditions. As Joshua Cohen has put it,

> the fact that individuals have an *interest* in improving their material situation, and are intelligent enough to devise ways of doing it, does *not* so far provide them with an interest in *improving the forces of production*. Only under *specific structural* conditions is the interest in material advantage tied to an interest in a strategy of productivity-enhancing investment. (J. Cohen, 1982, p. 268)

But the problem does not only lie in taking for granted that a rational desire to overcome scarcity is immediately transposed into improved technology. Even if one were hypothetically to accept that Cohen's argument works in reality or even if one were to limit one's analysis to those societies and epochs in which a constant development of productive forces is clearly detectable, there would still be a problem with Cohen's inference that relations of production are functionally accounted for by their tendency to enhance the growth of productive forces. For despite systematic and consistent technical change there is no guarantee that the class opposition derived from the structure of relations of production will effectively bring about a change in the mode of production and, specifically, there is no guarantee that the revolutionary class which has the interest in transforming the production relations will be able to do so. As Levine and Wright have pointed out, 'there is no simple, monolithic relation between technical change and the growth in the class capacities of the working class' (1980, p. 66).

It should be obvious by now that the problems I have been discussing are not exclusive to Cohen's version of historical materialism but in their more basic features also affect the general orthodox account of the primacy of productive forces. It is true that Cohen compounds the problem by deriving the social from the material and by narrowly defining productive forces in purely material terms. But even if one takes a wider concept of productive forces as comprising work relations and even if one considers productive forces as a part of the mode of production it is still true that the orthodox approach attempts to explain change and the character of production relations by the development of productive forces which, for whatever reasons, is taken for granted. It is surprising how little attention Soviet orthodoxy and other technological determinisms pay to Marx's numerous analyses of non-European societies, where one of the main features underlined is the stationary character of their productive forces. From his early letters and articles on India and China to the mature analyses of pre-capitalist economic formations in the *Grundrisse* and *Capital* a consistent view is developed which characterizes Asiatic societies in very different terms from those used to explain the development of Western Europe.

In effect, referring to India in a letter to Engels, Marx speaks of the 'stationary character of this part of Asia − despite all the pointless movement on the political surface' and sees in the village system the 'solid foundation for Asiatic despotism and stagnation' which could only be broken by the external imposition of British rule (14 June 1853, MESC, pp. 79–80). Marx's articles on India insist that 'however changing the political aspect of India's past must appear, its social condition has remained unaltered since its remotest antiquity' and that the structural pivots of such a society are 'the hand-loom and the spinning-wheel' from immemorial times (AOIC, SFE, p. 304). Forcefully arguing against any romantic view of village life, he reminds his readers that these communities were contaminated by caste and slavery and that 'they transformed a self-developing social state into never-changing natural destiny' (p. 306). Apart from successive conquests 'Indian society has no history at all' because each new empire was founded 'on the passive basis of that unresisting and unchanging society' (p. 320).

In *Capital* Marx carries on the same, though more detailed, analysis of the economic life of the Indian communities, which is described in terms of an 'unalterable division of labour' (K, Vol.1, p. 337) and

the simplicity of the organisation for production in these self-sufficing communities that constantly reproduce themselves in the same form . . . this simplicity supplies the key to the secret of the unchangeableness of Asiatic societies, an unchangeableness in such striking contrast with the constant dissolution and refounding of Asiatic states, and the never-ceasing changes of dynasty. The structure of the economic elements of society remains untouched by the storm-clouds of the political sky. (K, Vol. 1, pp. 338–9)

In fact by the time Marx finished writing the *Grundrisse* he came to conceive the special features of these societies in terms of a different mode of production, the 'Asiatic mode of production', which is mentioned for the first and only time in the 1859 Preface. This mode of production is characterized by the lack of private ownership of the land, which is controlled by the state, and is based on self-sufficient villages, which pay tribute to a central state-power, which is typically in charge of big irrigation and hydraulic projects.

It would be a mistake to believe that Marx confined this idea of 'Asiatic societies' or the 'Asiatic mode of production' to geographically Asiatic countries. In fact Marx finds Asiatic features in pre-colonial America – especially Peru and Mexico – and Celtic and other tribal societies (see G, p. 473). A thorough survey of Marx's writings by Melotti shows that the list of countries and regions mentioned in connection with all or some of the Asiatic characteristics also includes – apart from India and China – Egypt, Mesopotamia, Persia, Arabia, Turkey, Tartary, Java, the Dutch East Indies, Russia, the Etruscans and Spain under the Moors (Melotti, 1982, p. 77). The sheer number and extension of regions referred to in the context of the Asiatic mode of production should have alerted Marxist authors to the fact that the primacy of productive forces, if at all valid, operates in a very restricted geographical space according to Marx's own account, and that therefore extreme caution should be exercised before erecting it as a universal principle of the history of humankind. In fact, as we saw in Chapter 2, Kolakowski has put forward the idea that orthodox Marxism, in the time of Stalin, excluded the 'Asiatic mode of production' precisely because it cast doubt about a universally valid theory of history whose main tenet was the idea of a uniform pattern of development everywhere propelled by the constant progress of productive forces (Kolakowski, 1978, Vol. 1, p. 350). Whether or not Kolakowski is right in believing that there was a conscious attempt to scrap an inconvenient theoretical element for reasons of expediency, it is still true that such a concept confronts Marxism with a problem which must be resolved and not avoided.

However, this does not mean that one must necessarily accept the notion of an Asiatic mode of production as an analytical tool with the same intellectual standing as the concepts of capitalist or feudal modes of production. In fact in recent years there has been an important controversy within Marxism between those who see in that concept the possibility of developing a multilinear conception of history which does not require the universal occurrence of feudalism (see for instance, Melotti, 1982, and Rey, 1978) and those who reject such a notion as untenable (see Anderson, 1979b, and Hindess and Hirst, 1975). There is indeed something very strange in a supposedly abstract analytical category, universally applicable, which is labelled 'Asiatic'. One gets the impression of a rag-bag concept where Marx dumped a series of different historical cases whose only common element seems to be the fact that they did not evolve towards capitalism as Western Europe did. Even defenders of the concept find it difficult to define the class structure which characterizes the Asiatic mode of production. Melotti, for instance, is aware of the problem of deciding who makes up the exploiting class, given the fact that there are two levels of 'exploitation' – within the village and between the village and the central state. He eventually decides that the central functionaries of the state (mandarins, bureaucrats and the military) constitute such a class which appropriates the rent from the land (Melotti, 1982, pp. 60–1). But then he has to recognize that Marx did not think of bureaucracy as a class and that one of the features of the Asiatic mode of production is the lack of private ownership of the means of production. Anderson is his turn argues that Marx relied on accounts of Asia which were the result of colonial misinterpretations and that, above all, the stationary character of oriental empires is an illusion. Thus he concludes that the Asiatic mode of production 'suffered the inherent weakness of functioning essentially as a generic residual category for non-European development' and thence proposes that such a notion 'be given the decent burial that it deserves' (Anderson, 1979b, pp. 488, 495 and 548).

Be this as it may, the point is not so much whether the concept of an Asiatic mode of production is intellectually sound but the fact that Marx conceived of many non-European societies as lacking the potential for autonomous development and requiring the 'revolutionary' external intervention of colonial powers in order to have a chance of developing their productive forces. As Marx put it in the case of India, 'England has to fulfil a double mission in India: one destructive, the other regenerating – the annihilation of old Asiatic society, and the laying of the material foundations of Western society in Asia' (AOIC, SFE, p. 320). The same idea seems to be in Marx and Engels's mind when they supported the North American invasion of Mexico and in general the North American expansion to the Pacific Ocean. As Engels put it:

> In *America* we have witnessed the conquest of Mexico, which has pleased us. It constitutes progress too that a country until the present day exclusively occupied with itself, torn apart by perpetual civil wars and prevented from all development, a country which at best was on the verge of falling under the industrial vassalage of England, that such a country be thrown by means of violence into the historical movement. It is in the interest of its own development that Mexico will be in the future under the tutelage of the United States. It is in the interest of the development of all America that the United States, by means of the occupation of California, obtain predominance over the Pacific ocean. (DB,MHAL, 1979, p. 183)

Of course, it can be argued that Marx was absolutely mistaken about this not only because his assessment of the role of colonialism was over-optimistic but also because, as Anderson has tried to show, the 'stationary' character of Asiatic societies is a myth. It is true that Marx did not deny the existence of substantial political changes in those societies but he certainly denied that they affected the economic structure and, by implication, a static system of production relations means static productive forces. Anderson has shown on the contrary that forces of production did grow in Imperial China and so much that 'most of the purely technical pre-conditions for a capitalist industrialization were achieved far earlier in China than they were in Europe. China possessed a comprehensive and decisive technological lead over the occident by the later Middle Ages' (Anderson, 1979b, p. 54). According to this it could be argued that Marx's most general theory of history as the growth of productive forces is universally valid in spite of and in opposition to his rather Hegelian and Eurocentric remarks about 'peoples without history' and stationary economies. But then this argument does not hold much water either because China did not become capitalist and eventually, as Anderson himself recognizes, technological growth stopped or even went into reverse (ibid., p. 541).

In fact one of the conclusions which Anderson draws from his historical analysis of the end of European feudalism is that

> contrary to widely received beliefs among Marxists – the characteristic 'figure' of a crisis in a mode of production is not one in which vigorous (economic) forces of production burst triumphantly through retrograde (social) relations of production, and promptly establish a higher productivity and society on their ruins. On the contrary, the forces of production typically tend to *stall* and *recede* within the existent relations of production; these then must themselves first be radically changed and reordered *before* new forces of production can be created and combined for a globally new mode of production. (Anderson, 1978, p. 204)

It is therefore rather surprising to find that in a subsequent work Anderson seems fully to endorse Cohen's technological conception (see Anderson, 1980, pp. 55 and 65). Whatever one thinks of this change of position it is quite obvious that Anderson's example of China shows that even if productive forces develop and change this does not necessarily result in the expected changes in production relations as the primacy thesis implies. Hence, although Marx may have overemphasized the stationary character of non-European countries, the mere fact that apparently similar levels of technological development may bring about absolutely different production relations and that therefore the development of non-European societies does not necessarily follow the same pattern as the European development calls in question the universal primacy of productive forces. Why then was Marx so emphatic in asserting the primacy of productive forces in his general theoretical statements about history? Two elements seem to be important in answering this question. First, because capitalism was his main object of analysis, Marx tended to generalize the crucial role which productive forces performed in its expansion and did not realize the theoretical consequences of his own analyses of other modes of production, fragmentary and scattered though they may have been. Second, Marx was certainly influenced by and to a certain extent shared the nineteenth century's belief in the continuous progress of science and technology.

We have already seen how the Third International in 1928 reversed its own original position, which had followed Marx's positive assessment of the results of imperialism. From that moment onwards the orthodox line is to affirm that imperialism is an obstacle to the development of productive forces. Yet just as Marx was mistaken in his belief that non-European societies were fundamentally static in their productive forces and that colonial intervention was bound to be beneficial to these countries because it would result in their industrialization, so is the new orthodoxy mistaken in its belief that productive forces would naturally progress and follow the European pattern were it not for imperialism, which prevents them from doing so. Marx's position is today represented by Warren (1980) while Baran (1957) and Frank (1969) take the new orthodox and opposite view. The experience of the so-called underdeveloped countries, particularly after the Second World War, shows that imperialism neither resulted in the full industrialization of backward regions nor absolutely impeded their development. As Cardoso and Faletto have argued, dependent development or dependent industrialization processes are possible which show that productive forces are neither stagnant nor self-propelling (Cardoso and Faletto, 1979).

The first consequence of rejecting the primacy of productive forces is a necessary shift of emphasis in explaining social change in antagonistic societies from the structural contradiction between forces and relations of production to class struggle. Orthodox accounts normally give to class struggle a derived and subordinate status, entirely dependent on 'structural' factors. Anderson, for example, after his endorsement of Cohen, rejects as a facile 'temptation' the idea that upheaval and disorder are the province of class struggle and that crises are identical with class confrontations: 'the *onset* of major economic crises, whether under feudalism or capitalism, has typically taken all social classes unawares, deriving from structural depths below those of direct conflict between them' (Anderson, 1980, p. 55). It is difficult to understand how it is possible within Marxism to separate the origin of crises from class struggles. Crises are by definition an expression of the fundamental contradiction of a mode of production (TSV, Vol. 2, p. 500). The contradiction between capital and labour, for instance, entails a relation between proletariat and bourgeoisie by its form, and the extraction of surplus-value by means of the production of commodities by its content. In a crisis, therefore, the same basic contradiction manifests itself both as an economic problem in the production of commodities and the realization of surplus-value on the one hand and as class struggle on the other. It is the result of the latter that determines how the economic problem is tackled. The fact that classes may not be fully aware or conscious at the onset of the crisis does not imply the absence of class struggle at the centre of the crisis. Just as Anderson, following Cohen, criticized Thompson for incorporating consciousness in the definition of class positions (Cohen, 1978, p. 73; Anderson, 1980, p. 40), he should have realized that class struggle too does not necessarily depend on the full awareness of the classes involved (see Ste Croix, 1983, p. 60, and 1984, p. 100).

The second consequence is the necessary abandonment of the unilinear theory of history as a series of stages through which all nations must travel. There is no uniform pattern of development propelled by a universal mechanism. The European historical evolution described by Marx in terms of a certain succession of modes of production does not apply everywhere nor is there any universal necessity in that particular sequence. This is perhaps the single most common criticism of the Marxist theory of history, and is elaborated in various forms by critics such as Popper (1973, pp. 82 and 107), Leff (1961, pp. 104–6), Kolakowski (1978, Vol. 1, pp. 365–6), Bober (1968, pp. 326–8), Acton (1954, pp. 168–71), Hook (1955, p. 36) and recently Giddens (1981, pp. 1, 2 and 20–3). But few of them seem to be aware that Marx himself explicitly rejected the transformation of his historical sketch of the genesis of capitalism in Western Europe 'into an historico-philosophical theory of the general path of development prescribed by fate to all nations' (Letter, November 1877, MESC, p. 293). It is surprising how ready critics are to conflate Marx with Marxist orthodoxy. Even when critics are aware of the existence of tensions in Marx's thought, they invariably tend to resolve them in the orthodox sense.

Since the times of Plekhanov orthodoxy has always been careful not to confuse determinism with fatalism, which entails passivity and neglect of human political intervention in social processes. Historical necessity asserts itself but it does so only through the actions of human beings, who are therefore 'instruments of this necessity' (Plekhanov, 1976b pp. 13–14). However, although Marxist orthodoxy cannot be accused of forgoing human practice and class struggle, its conception of practice as an 'instrument of necessity' is open to criticism. First, because as I have already shown, one cannot derive from the fact of human rationality the fact that human beings are going to take a precise course of action, or, as other critics have put it, the existence of a general class interest in the transformation of society does not of itself entail that such a class possesses the capacities to transform society. Second, because in conceiving practice as an instrument of necessity orthodoxy reduces it to a more or less automatic or mechanical activity which human beings are not free to control or change. It is not only that human beings 'cannot help desiring' (Plekhanov) to serve as instruments of necessity and that, therefore, they are supposed to be programmed to want certain goals like the 'cultural dopes' criticized by Giddens (1981, p. 18). It is also that, given the assumption that what they desire automatically sets in motion an effective political practice bound to achieve it, this practice appears to be as absolutely predetermined as the theatrical roles which actors must perform. It is true that human beings are conditioned by material circumstances independent of their will. Yet this does not mean that they are bound to act in a particular direction, even if one can prove that they have a real interest in doing so. The determination of material conditions certainly gives rise to a task whose solution is possible but which cannot guarantee its own successful accomplishment.

4

Some Elements for the Reconstruction of Historical Materialism

I have already affirmed that there is a need to reconstruct historical materialism as a theory of practice in opposition to a deterministic and teleological interpretation which reduces social evolution to a process of natural history regulated by ineluctable laws. The basic idea behind this attempt was put forward by Marx himself when he stated that 'men make their own history, but they do not make it just as they please; they do not make it under circumstances chosen by themselves, but under circumstances directly encountered, given and transmitted from the past' (BRUM, MESW, p. 96). This idea is complemented by Marx's expressed belief that 'circumstances are changed by men' and that 'the coincidence of the changing of circumstances and of human activity or self-change can be conceived and rationally understood only as *revolutionary practice*' (TOF, 3, GI, p. 4). It is necessary to explore the meaning of these ideas in greater detail in order to see whether they can become the key to the resolution of those tensions I have identified in Marx and Engels's thought.

Marx started with the idea that 'all social life is essentially practical. All mysteries which lead theory to mysticism find their rational solution in human practice and in the comprehension of this practice' (TOF, 8, GI, p. 5). It is highly significant that in Marx and Engels's first formulation of historical materialism the concept of practice plays a pivotal role. In describing the premisses from which historical materialism must begin Marx and Engels affirm that 'they are the real individuals, their activity and the material conditions of their life, both those which they find already existing and those produced by their activity' (GI, p. 31). Human beings must first produce the means to reproduce their material life. But this appears as a twofold relation: 'on the one hand as a natural, on the other as a social relation – social in the sense that it denotes the co-operation of several individuals' (GI, p. 43). This co-operation is regulated by particular political and legal arrangements and is sustained by specific beliefs and forms of consciousness.

Practice is intentional and purposive activity which not only transforms nature but also transforms human beings themselves. Practice reproduces the physical life of individuals but is is also 'a definite form of expressing their life, a definite *mode of life* on their part' (GI, p. 31). Society as a whole is the result of practice. As Marx put it, 'what is society, whatever its form may be? The product of men's reciprocal action.' But he immediately adds an important rider: 'are men free to choose this or that form of society? By no means' (letter to P. V. Annenkov, 28 December 1846, MESC, p. 30). This means that although practice is the basic social fact it is not absolutely free or unconditioned. In fact human practices crystallize themselves into an 'objective power', objectify themselves into structures and social relations which human beings up to the capitalist mode of production have not controlled. These objectifications of practice set limits to actual human practices. This is the sense of Marx's saying that men make history but not just as they please.

Marxist theory wants to steer clear of conceiving practice as either the free action of undetermined individuals or the totally predetermined activity of mere agents. Structuralist theories of action conceive of human beings not as real actors of history but rather as agents of forces and relations which they do not control. Thus for Althusser practices are structured in set patterns or structures, of which human beings are only the bearers or supporters (1971, p. 158). At the opposite extreme actionalist theories of action conceive of individuals as the free actors of history and underrate the determination of their actions. Sartre for instance, bases his theory of practice on the universality of the individual (1968, p. 57) and this is related to his existentialism, for which individual consciousness is the basis of radical freedom (see Poster, 1979, p. 22). Whereas for Althusser the structures are constitutive and subjects are constituted, for Sartre the subject is constitutive and the structures are constituted. They thus pull apart subject and object, the unity of which Marx tried to safeguard precisely by means of the concept of practice.

One can see now why practice is so central a concept for historical materialism: it constitutes the meeting point of and the unity between human beings and nature, the social and the material, subjects and structures, consciousness and reality. Practice appears as labour but also as self-expression, as physical reproduction but also as social reproduction, as material activity but also as social activity, as reproduction of social relations but also as political transformation of social relations. As Kosik has put it, 'in the concept of praxis, socio-human reality is discovered as the opposite of givenness, i.e. at once as the process of forming human *being* and as its specific form. *Praxis is the sphere of the human being*' (1976, p. 136). The inclusiveness of practice in Marx's treatment underlines its centrality for historical materialism but it is also the source of its problems as an analytical concept. All-encompassing concepts which entail several dimensions have two main difficulties. On the one hand they tend to be vague and lack precision, on the other they can easily be reduced to only one of their dimensions to the exclusion of others. I have already mentioned examples of reductionism in the conceptions of Sartre and Althusser. Marx himself has been accused by Habermas (1972, and 1982, p. 268) and Wellmer (1971) of reducing practice to instrumental action and of disregarding communicative interaction. This is why Habermas contends that subjects do not 'produce' their social life-context in the same fashion as they make commodities and Wellmer rejects the idea that the realm of freedom is 'produced' according to the pattern of instrumental action.

It is indeed true that Marx fused into the same concept two forms of human activity which the Greeks had distinguished as *praxis* and *poiesis*. *Praxis* for the Greeks was mainly political or artistic activity. *Poiesis* was the material activity of producing or making something. So when the Greeks distinguished between theory and praxis they did not refer to thinking as different from acting but rather to two styles of life: contemplative life and political life. For Aristotle 'practical life is the life of active citizenship, of active participation in the life of the *Polis*. Theoretical life on the contrary is a life of detachment from political partnership' (Lobkowicz, 1967, p. 5). However, the fact that Marx subsumed both *praxis* and *poiesis* in the concept of practice does not necessarily mean that he reduced practice to *poiesis* or instrumental action as Habermas and Wellmer contend. True, Marx emphasizes labour as fundamental because it is the process whereby human beings create their material existence. In the *Paris Manuscripts* he praises Hegel for grasping the nature of labour and conceiving objective man 'as the result of his own labour' (EPM, EW, p. 386). But Marx was quite aware that although labour is a fundamental dimension of practice it is not of itself necessarily liberating. This is why in the same context he criticizes Hegel because 'he sees only the positive and not the negative side of labour' (p. 386).

By means of labour human beings satisfy their needs and overcome the constraints of nature; yet, as labour takes place under specific social conditions and circumstances produced but not necessarily chosen or controlled by human beings, it can become alienating and degrading. For Marx productive labour in so far as is a continuous process does not only reproduce itself but reproduces also the alienated and contradictory social relations under which it takes place: 'capitalist production, therefore under its aspect of a continuous connected process, of a process of reproduction, produces not only commodities, not only surplus-value, but it also produces and reproduces the *capitalist relation*; on the one side the capitalist on the other the *wage-labourer*' (K. Vol. 1, p. 575). So it is true that for Marx the production of social reality cannot be detached from labour. There is no specific practice separated from labour that is able to construct basic relations of production. But Marx never considered labour to be exclusively positive and inherently capable of bringing about liberation. This is why he also gives fundamental importance to the 'change of circumstances' which should be conceived as 'revolutionary practice' (TOF, 3, GI, p. 4).

Although Marx's distinction between labour and revolutionary practice covers the two more basic dimensions of practice it does not exhaust all of them. Labour is certainly the main form of reproductive practice but within the capitalist mode of production there is also a reproductive practice which is specifically political and is oriented to the maintenance and legal protection of the existing social relations of production. Similarly, there are different forms of revolutionary practice. Some may seek political power without altering productive relations. For Marx, on the contrary, the change of relations of production is of the essence of his kind of revolutionary practice. Furthermore, there are other differences which separate, say, a peasant revolt of the sixteenth century in Germany and the Bolshevic revolution of 1917. Each historical epoch and the diversity of its modes of production fix specific parameters and potentialities for human practice. It is through the practical deployment of human beings that history is made. But human practice does not remain the same.

At the beginning of human history there hardly exists any form of individuation and political practice. As Marx put it, 'human beings become individuals only through the process of history. He appears originally as a *species-being, clan being, herd animal* – although in no way whatever as a *Zoon Politikon* in the political sense' (G, p. 496). Then, when forms of land property and of personal dependency emerge (slavery, feudalism), it is still impossible to conceive of labour and forms of exploitation as separate from political and religious considerations. Slave and peasant revolts could not fully understand the real character of social contradictions and so they formulated their radical programmes in religious terms and eventually facilitated the rule of classes other than themselves (see PWG). Political upheavals did not alter basic economic and social structures. With the emergence of capitalism personal independence is acquired but 'founded on *objective* dependence' (G, p. 158). For the first time labour and political practices become clearly distinguished and the importance of the productive system can be theoretically appreciated. According to Marx this is the precondition for the proletariat to become involved in a fully conscious revolutionary practice which seeks to abolish the class system itself. Whereas the bourgeois revolution had been a political extension of economic changes occurring beforehand, now Marx propounds a political revolution which has to change the economy. Up to the end of the capitalist mode of production it is possible to speak of an 'alienated practice' in so far as social relations are not yet under communal control. Assuming the success of revolutionary practice in transforming social relations of production, it is possible to speak of a 'liberated practice' in as much as the new social relations are subordinated to the individuals's communal control.

It is very important not to conceive of revolutionary practice as 'free activity' in opposition to labour as 'necessary activity'. Revolutionary practice is also conditioned by social and economic structures, yet it is not the automatic result of those circumstances. Revolutionary practice is neither arbitrary nor absolutely prefigured. In *The German Ideology* Marx argues that the domination of material circumstances over individuals sets them the task of transforming such dependence 'into the control and conscious mastery of these powers' (GI, p. 51). Yet Marx is equally clear that human beings are not necessarily bound to accomplish the task. This is why he can affirm that 'communism is for us not a *state of affairs* which is to be established, an *ideal* to which reality (will) have to adjust itself. We call communism the *real* movement which abolishes the present state of things' (GI, p. 49). In this sense revolutionary practice mediates between necessity and freedom.

CHARACTER AND SCOPE OF HISTORICAL MATERIALISM

The concept of practice has two important consequences for historical materialism. First, it specifies the theoretical nature of historical materialism and the historical character of its object. Second, it determines the crucial role of material production and particularly of the capitalist mode of production for the understanding of history. In the first place historical materialism affirms the connection between theory and history. Yet this does not mean that it is about the writing of history in the sense of a narration of past events. Historiography is not the same as history. Historiography is concerned with the interpretation of and writing about past events; history is about a global process whereby human beings practically construct their lives, involving not only the past but also the present and the future. Historical materialism is certainly concerned with understanding the past, although not necessarily with narrating historical events in their particularity; but, above all, historical materialism is about understanding the present in order to change it and so shape the future. Hence historical materialism is neither a theory separated from history (Althusser and Balibar, 1975, p. 105; Hindess and Hirst, 1975, p. 317) nor historiography separated from theory (Thompson, 1978, pp. 223 and 236).

When I say that historical materialism is a theory about history I mean that it is an attempt to elaborate the categories which can be applied to understand social formations within the domain of history. Historical materialism is certainly not a general philosophy or transcendental account of the necessary course of history but it is concerned with history in the sense that it constructs the concepts necessary to render historical processes intelligible. This means that, like all theories, historical materialism uses abstraction to constitute its concepts. But this abstractive process is not detached from the observational level, it must be carried out in correspondence with it (see Willer and Willer, 1973, p. 20).

Thompson is right when he argues against Althusser that historical materialism is not an independent philosophy or theory separated from history (1978, p. 236). Yet he does not seem to realize that as a theory historical materialism cannot simply arise from the observation of historical events by means of a process of generalization. As a theory historical materialism requires abstract concepts, not in the sense of a conjunction of generalizations derived from different sets of observations but in the sense of non-observable constructs which are related with one another in order to explain observable historical phenomena. No particular observation of a succession of historical events can of itself generate abstract concepts such as productive forces, relations of production, class, surplus-value and their interconnections. This does not mean that these concepts and their theoretical relationships are constructed in isolation from historical events, as Hindess and Hirst contend (1975, pp. 310, 312 and 317); they must correspond to, but they are not the mere result of, empirical observations. This is why one cannot assimilate historical materialism to historiography or conceive the former as a direct product of the latter.

It can be argued that the status of 'general theories' is suspect and that Marx himself rejected the study of general categories such as 'production in general' or 'labour in general'. For instance, he asserts that 'whenever we speak of production, then, what is meant is always production at a definite stage of social development' (Introduction, G, p. 85), and referring to the general elements of the process of labour he insists that 'as the taste of the porridge does not tell you who grew the oats, no more does this simple process tell you of itself what are the social conditions under which it is taking place' (K, Vol. 1, p. 179). From this it is possible to conclude, as Poulantzas does, that a general theory of the economy, the state or the superstructures is impossible because their theoretical objects are not invariant. What is possible and legitimate is a theory of the capitalist economy or the feudal economy but not a general theory (Poulantzas, 1978, pp. 17–24). Poulantzas does not elaborate the consequences of this position for historical materialism and limits himself to saying that one of the merits of Marxism is to have rejected the 'vague, smoky, general and abstract theories which pretend to revealing the great secrets of History, Politics, the State and Power' (p. 22).

It seems to me that this kind of argument contains a confusion. It is necessary to distinguish the notion of a general theory from the conception of the object of a theory as an object in general, that is to say, an object abstracted from specific historical determinations. To speak of a 'general theory of society' is not the same as speaking of a 'theory of society in general'. Marx would never have denied the general theoretical character of historical materialism but he would have rejected the conception of historical materialism as a theory of society in general. Even more, only a general theory of historical materialism can propose the idea that one cannot study production, labour or society in general, without reference to specific historical determinations. The general theoretical status of historical materialism has to do with the character of scientific abstraction and the elaboration of non-observable concepts in order to understand specific historical societies. What is to be rejected is not this necessary general theoretical character but the reduction of its object to a general category. The consequence of such a reduction is the mistaken attempt to derive the particular concrete from the general abstract and to substitute a suprahistorical logical account for historical analysis.

Of course, Marx does not deny that all societies, all epochs of production and labour, have certain elements in common and therefore the general concepts of labour, production or society, as 'rational abstractions', are useful because they fix the common aspects and save us repetition (Introduction, G, p. 85). But in order to understand the specificity of each form of society Marx asserts the primacy of those determinations which are not common. One cannot understand a particular historical phase of society by deducing it from the concept of society in general as if the former were a mere specific logical combination of invariant elements inherent in the latter. As Marx put it: 'There are characteristics which all stages of production have in common, and which are established as general ones by the mind; but the so-called *general preconditions* of all production are nothing more than these abstract moments with which no real historical stage of production can be grasped' (Introduction, G, p. 88). In addition to these general concepts which cover elements common to all epochs, other abstract concepts are required which capture the elements which are not general and common. Therefore it is possible to affirm that there is no contradiction between the general theoretical character of historical materialism and the historical character of its object.

I have already affirmed the connection between historical materialism and history, understood not in the sense of historiography but in the sense of a process whereby human beings practically produce their material conditions of life. This is what Marx and Engels call 'the first premise of all human history', namely, the fact that human beings produce their material life by means of their activity and 'distinguish themselves from animals as soon as they begin to *produce* their means of subsistence' (GI, p. 31). In this manner Marx and Engels assert the crucial importance of production for understanding history. Thus Marx starts his 1857 Introduction with 'The object before us, to begin with, *material production*' (G, p. 83). Yet the 1857 Introduction goes further than *The German Ideology* in that it introduces two important methodological points as to how production should be studied. The first, which I have already mentioned, has to do with the idea that historical materialism cannot start from the concept of production in general but must grasp production 'in definite historical form' (TSV, Vol. 1, p. 285). The second point clarifies the first and has to do with the idea that historical materialism cannot start from the most primitive systems of production but must analyse first the most advanced in order to be able to understand the former.

In so far as the first point is concerned, Marx introduces the concept of mode of production as the key category in analysing production in historical form. Unfortunately he does not precisely define it, nor does he clarify its relation to specific historical societies. The nearest to a definition of mode of production is found in the *Grundrisse*: 'a specific *mode of production* . . . which appears both as a relation between the individuals, and as their specific active relation to inorganic nature, a specific mode of working' (G, p. 495). This suggests the basic correctness of those versions which describe the mode of production as the combination of productive forces and relations of production (Lange, 1974, p. 17; Melotti, 1982, p. 3; Laclau, 1969, p. 282, and 1977, p. 34). It is important to understand the abstract nature of this concept. As Laclau has put it, a mode of production is 'not a stage of concrete historical development. There is, therefore, no historical transformation that can be explained *exclusively* by unfolding the internal logic of a determinate mode of production' (Laclau, 1977, p. 42). Historical societies or 'social formations' usually contain various modes of production, one of which is dominant. (Note that I do not follow here the Leninist notion of socioeconomic formation as a historical epoch or period, but understand by it a concrete historical society.) Historical changes occur in specific social formations and are explained with the help of the concept of mode of production. But the former are not simply deducible from the economic logic of the latter (Bertrand, 1979, pp. 56–7).

Marx never clarified this relation in a satisfactory fashion. Indeed, he was on occasions guilty of confusing the two levels. Sometimes one is led to believe that the logic of the mode of production suffices to understand how and when that mode is going to change or develop. Yet the analysis of the transformations of a mode of production can only be carried out at the level of a social formation. This is why history cannot be conceived as a necessary succession of modes of production. This has important consequences for historical materialism and historical analysis. For instance, in abstract, the capitalist mode of production is supposed to bring about an explosive increase of productive forces. But, in the concrete situation of a historical social formation, the capitalist mode of prodution can exhaust its potentiality at a very early stage, depending on its articulation with other modes of production and specific historical circumstances such as imperialism. Thus Marx and Engels had to recognize that in the case of Ireland British imperialism had 'destroyed all industrial life' and hindered her development, which was the opposite to the position they had taken earlier on with regard to India and China. Another case in point is the dependent capitalism of contemporary underdeveloped countries. So, apart from other problems, Marx's idea that no social system perishes before its social productive forces develop fully cannot be applied at the level of the mode of production but makes sense within the specific historical circumstances of a social formation, with its particular arrangement of modes of production and international relations. This may partly explain why socialist revolutions have succeeded where the capitalist mode of production was impeded by very resilient pre-capitalist modes of production or colonial rule. But, although this may make more sense than the traditional position which refers that dictum to the mode of production, there is still a problem with the idea that social change or socialist revolutions are caused by the development or exhaustion of productive forces.

In so far as the second point is concerned, Marx propounds

the idea that historical materialism should start by studying capitalist production, which will provide the key to understand early productive systems:

> Bourgeois society is the most developed and the most complex historic organization of production. The categories which express its relations, the comprehension of its structure, thereby also allows insights into the structure and the relations of production of all the vanished social formations . . . Human anatomy contains a key to the anatomy of the ape. The intimations of higher development among the subordinate animal species, however, can be understood only after the higher development is already known. The bourgeois economy thus supplies the key to the ancient. (Introduction, G, p. 105)

This is so because it is only under the capitalist mode of production that the realization of the determinant role of production can occur in so far as for the first time production is disentangled from religious, political and kinship institutions and becomes a specialized sphere on its own. This allows the development of concepts and categories which could not have been produced as such before.

Take for example the concept of value. Marx asks why not even Aristotle, a great thinker, could conceive of it in ancient Greece. His answer is that

> to attribute value to commodities . . . is merely a mode of expressing all labour as equal human labour, and consequently as labour of equal quality. Greek society was founded upon slavery, and had, therefore, for its natural basis, the inequality of men and of their labour-powers. The secret of the expression of value, namely, that all kinds of labour are equal and equivalent, because, and so far as they are human labour in general, cannot be deciphered, until the notion of human equality has already acquired the fixity of a popular prejudice. This, however, is possible only in a society in which the great mass of the produce of labour takes the form of commodities. (K, Vol. 1, p. 65).

This is related to the fact that the expropriation of surplus labour can only be conceived as such once the capitalist economic appropriation of surplus labour arises in history, for it is only within capitalism that a disjunction can be determined between the equivalence of exchange values in the market and the appropriation of surplus-value at the level of production.

This may seem paradoxical because the expropriation of surplus labour within capitalism is concealed by the appearances of the market whereas the expropriation of surplus labour within feudalism was quite apparent and surplus labour was precisely marked off from necessary labour. The point is, however, that as the economy was not an autonomous level of feudal society independent of religious and political institutions, the very concept of surplus labour did not make sense as an independent economic concept and could not have been arrived at without the notion of value and abstract labour. Feudalism as much as slavery, in so far as they are modes of production, can only be properly understood when the emergence of capitalism allows the development of the essential categories to apprehend former productive systems. Nevertheless, this does not mean that historical materialism should foist onto the past institutions and relations which are only typical of capitalism. Marx is careful to point out that capitalist production supplies the key to the ancient 'but not at all in the manner of those economists who smudge over all historical differences and see bourgeois relations in all forms of society' (Introduction, G, p. 105). Capitalist economic relations allow the understanding of feudal and slave relations but one must not identify them with one another.

Sometimes it is believed that the real object of Marx's theory was exclusively capitalist society for the simple reason that there is no systematic treatment of former productive systems other than scattered fragments and references written for purposes of comparison in the analysis of the capitalist mode of production. Yet the fact that Marx was able to complete only his studies of capitalist production does not mean that he abandoned historical materialism and the project of studying other modes of production. As he put it, 'these indications, together with a correct grasp of the present, then also offer the key to the understanding of the past – a work in its own right which, it is to be hoped, we shall be able to undertake as well' (G, p. 461). However, the fact that historical materialism can only be developed by starting from and as the result of the emergence of capitalism has been interpreted by some authors, both Marxist and non-Marxist, as meaning that it is relevant to and can apply only to capitalism. Lukács, for instance, conceives of historical materialism as 'the self-knowledge of capitalist society', as an ideological weapon which is, 'in the first instance, a theory of bourgeois society and its economic structure' (Lukács, 1971, p. 229). True, as a scientific method historical materialism can also be applied to former societies but 'a weighty methodological difficulty makes itself felt' which lies 'in the structural difference between the age of civilization and the epochs that preceded it' (p. 232).

In order to illustrate this structural difference Lukács quotes the famous passage where Marx contends that 'in all forms in which landed property is the decisive factor, natural relations still predominate; in the forms in which the decisive factor is capital, social, historically evolved elements predominate' (Introduction, G, p. 107, but this translation is taken from CCPE, p. 213). More recently, in his critique of historical materialism Giddens argues that 'in non-capitalist societies co-ordination of authoritative resources forms the determining axis of societal integration and change. In capitalism, by contrast, allocative resources take on a very particular significance' (Giddens, 1981, p. 4; see also pp. 105 and 109). From this he concludes that in so far as historical materialism propounds the primacy of allocative resources it should be discarded as an overall theory of history.

I do not find these arguments compelling. From the fact that historical materialism must start its analysis with capitalist production it does not necessarily follow that it should be confined to capitalism. The very passage from Marx which Lukács quotes in support of restricting the scope of historical materialism proposes a theoretical distinction which is a *general conclusion of historical materialism itself!* It is the general theory of historical materialism that puts forward the thesis that natural relations predominate up to capitalism and that sociohistorical creations predominate from then onwards. It is historical materialism that proposes the historical character of categories and concepts and attempts to explain the crucial differences between pre-capitalist and capitalist societies. Besides, when Marx draws these distinctions he is not describing a primitive ahistorical society, where relations are not practically produced by human beings, in opposition to historical capitalist society, where human beings produce their relations. Marx is merely contrasting a kind of society where human beings do not control and have no power over relations they have themselves produced and a kind of society where, for the first time, human beings can become conscious and try to control their relations.

Giddens is right when he affirms the importance of force for the extraction of surplus production in pre-capitalist societies. Surplus-value is extracted by economic means alone only in capitalist societies. But from this it does not follow that authoritative resources alone are the central basis of power in pre-capitalist societies. There would be no power over persons without the possession of land which defines specific social relations. For Marx it is quite clear that 'the individuals in such a society, although their relations appear to be more personal, enter into connection with one another only as individuals imprisoned within a certain definition, as feudal lord and vassal, landlord and serf, etc.' (G, p. 163). To understand the central basis of power in pre-capitalist societies in terms of the primacy of authoritative resources begs the question. The point is to explain on what basis power or control over persons is achieved. This is not a purely arbitrary process. Otherwise, to the question of who has power in pre-capitalist society, the only answer would be: those who happen to have power. As Bottomore has pointed out, 'this is scarcely illuminating; it does not tell us how these particular individuals come to occupy the positions of power' (1964, p. 32; see also Wright, 1983).

PRACTICE AND THE RESOLUTION OF TENSIONS IN MARX'S THOUGHT

I started with the idea that a reconstructed historical materialism would have to resolve some tensions which were present in the thought of Marx and Engels themselves. I showed how orthodoxy gave a certain resolution to those tensions by proposing a conception of historical materialism which is supposedly derived from universal laws of dialectic inherent in nature, which conceives of consciousness as a mere reflection of matter, which considers technological progress as the main cause of social change and which results in an unilinear and teleological conception of historical development. The critique of this orthodox interpretation in Chapter 3 provides, even if only negatively and by contrast, the first elements of a different solution. I shall not repeat them here, but it is necessary to state in a more positive, if brief, fashion the way in which the theory of practice may contribute new resolutions of the tensions above mentioned.

In so far as the concept of dialectic is concerned it must be affirmed that when Marx described his own conception as an inversion of Hegel's he misunderstood the real nature of his own theory. Although I do not accept the Althusserian premiss that there is a systematic displacement between Marx's real theory and his own understanding of it, I propose that on this specific point Marx was mistaken in believing that it was only a matter of turning Hegelian dialectic right side up. The reason for this is connected with the concept of practice. For Hegel the production of thought was simultaneously the production of reality as its opposite, which means that the process of objectification (production of the object) was at the same time a process of alienation of consciousness: objectivity was the inverted creation of consciousness. Marx rejected the identification of objectification and alienation. The objective social world is produced by material practice. Human practice crystallizes itself not only in material products necessary for life, but also in social relations and institutions. This objectification of human practice is not of itself alienating. Alienation comes from what Marx described in *The German Ideology* as a 'limited material mode of activity' (GI, p. 36), which, although it produces the objective social world, does not control it.

Alienation has to do with the lack of human control of the results of human practice, not with the simple fact that human practice objectifies itself in certain results. Thus in alienation an inversion operates: the objective conditions which are practically produced govern their producers; the subjects become objects and vice versa. It is this idea of inversion which is at the centre of the notion of contradiction. But, whereas for Hegel inversion is necessarily given in any process of objectification, for Marx inversion occurs only within specific social conditions where a 'limited material mode of activity' is predominant. Consequently, for Hegel contradiction becomes the essence of all things which are the product of the self-alienation of consciousness. For Marx, on the contrary, contradiction emerges where human beings do not control the objective relations and institutions they themselves have practically produced, which means that the process of objectification, the reproduction of material life,

> appears as a process of dispossession from the standpoint of labour or as appropriation of alien labour from the standpoint of capital . . . But obviously this process of inversion is a merely *historical* necessity, a necessity for the development of the forces of production solely from a specific historic point of departure, or basis, but in no way an *absolute* necessity of production; rather, a vanishing one, and the result and the inherent purpose of this process is to suspend this basis itself. (G, pp. 831–2)

So, for a reconstructed historical materialism, contradiction is not the universal law of motion nor can social dialectic be derived from a natural dialectic. Dialectical development is a phase of history which Marx saw coming to an end as the consequence of the abolition of classes and of human beings finally controlling their relations. As he put it, 'universally developed individuals, whose social relations, as their own communal relations, are hence also subordinated to their own communal control, are no product of nature, but of history' (G, p. 162). This also means that the resolution of contradictions has to do with the actions of individuals themselves and not with natural or structural processes conceived as separate from human practice, which can supposedly liberate human beings from without. Human practice is thus involved in both the emergence and the resolution of contradictions. A limited material mode of activity gives rise to contradictions; revolutionary practice, in so far as it devolves control of social relations to the community, resolves the contradiction. This was never fully possible before capitalism because the resolution of contradictions was necessarily partial in that it only gave way to a new contradiction. Marx's point is that the proletariat is in a position not only to eliminate the specific capitalist contradiction by defeating the bourgeoisie, but also to abolish itself as a class, thus finally abolishing the class system itself: 'the condition for the emancipation of the working class is the abolition of all classes' (PP, p. 161).

The analysis of consciousness in terms of reflection, which is suggested by some of Marx and Engels's writings, has already been rejected for a good number of reasons, listed in Chapter 3, and the anticipatory character of consciousness has been upheld. Once more, the solution of this tension in Marx and Engels's thought is based upon the theory of practice. It is because reality should not be conceived 'in the form of the object' but as practice that consciousness cannot be understood as passive contemplation of a world already given but as an active process which accompanies and anticipates the practical constitution of reality. This means that human beings come to know reality in so far as they produce and appropriate that reality. Consciousness therefore not only 'reflects' but also 'anticipates' and 'projects'. Marx expressed this as follows:

the production of ideas, of conceptions, of consciousness, is at first directly interwoven with the material activity and the material intercourse of men – the language of real life. Conceiving, thinking, the mental intercourse of men at this stage still appear as the direct efflux of their material behaviour. The same applies to mental production as expressed in the language of the politics, laws, morality, religion, metaphysics, etc., of a people . . . Consciousness can never be anything else than conscious being, and the being of men is their actual life-process . . . men developing their material production and their material intercourse, alter, along with this their actual world, also their thinking and the products of their thinking. (GI, pp. 36–7)

In trying to understand consciousness in the context of practice Marx was separating himself from both Hegel and Feuerbach. For the former the production of thought had become the production of reality. For the latter reality was primary and thought was derivative. The treatment of consciousness in the context of practice means that consciousness is neither pure contemplation of a given world nor the creator of that world. True, there is a difference between the common-sense representations which human beings construct in their practical routines, and which allow them to manipulate their immediate environment, and the theoretical or scientific comprehension of reality which grasps what lies behind the appearances of that reality. Yet this difference, accepted and propounded by Marx, does not entail the detachment of science from practice. To Feuerbach's praise of the seemingly independent and contemplative approach of the natural sciences, which alone can disclose elements of reality that others cannot see, Marx retorts: 'where would natural science be without industry and commerce? Even this "pure" natural science is provided with an aim, as with its material, only through trade and industry, through the sensuous activity of men' (GI, p. 40).

The connection between consciousness and practice allows historical materialism to explain ideology and the social determination of consciousness in a manner which is more suggestive and better than the traditional way allowed by the base-superstructure metaphor. This metaphor is inevitably static, it tends to compartmentalize social reality into hypostasized levels, it tends to reify spheres of society which are thus taken as given and not as practically produced and, therefore, it tends to reduce dynamic phenomena such as consciousness or class struggle which pervade the whole of society to one specific level to the exclusion of others (see Williams, 1977, pp. 75–82).

It is important to understand that ideology and determination cannot be identified with one another. In the Mannheimian tradition it has become customary to assert that all social or historical knowledge is ideological in so far as it is socially determined. Determination is supposed to limit the claim to validity of any point of view because it relates thought to a particular and necessarily partial social position (Mannheim, 1972, p. 255). Historical materialism does not proceed in this way and its concept of ideology is much more restricted in scope. This is not the result of historical materialism being biased and one-sidedly criticizing others' points of view while refusing to accept its own social determination. For historical materialism the social determination of consciousness – which it certainly accepts in its own case – does not of itself affect the validity of ideas. It is true that all consciousness is socially determined but it is not true that all consciousness is ideological. For Marx and Engels ideology has to do with a specific kind of distorted consciousness which conceals social contradictions and thus objectively helps to reproduce them. Whence come these distorted ideas which mask contradictions? Again, the theory of practice offers an answer. We have already seen that all ideas are produced in the context of practice, but Marx goes further and finds that ideas can be a *real* or *illusory* expression of practice. As he puts it: 'ideas are the conscious expression – real or illusory – of their real relations and activities, of their production, of their intercourse, of their social and political conduct' (GI, p. 36). Ideology has to do with ideas which express practice inadequately. The reason for this is not a faulty cognitive process, but the limitations of practice itself: 'if the conscious expression of the real relations of these individuals is illusory, if in their imagination they turn reality upside-down, then this in its turn is the result of their *limited material mode of activity* and their limited social relations arising from it' (GI, p. 36, my emphasis).

These limitations of practice refer to the fact, already mentioned, that human beings produce a social world which they do not control, a 'fixation of social activity', a 'consolidation of what we ourselves produce into an objective power above us, growing out of our control' (GI, p. 47). This is the cause of 'inversions' or contradictions. In so far as human beings are unable practically to resolve these contradictions, in so far as they do not practically master such 'objective power', then they will seek to solve the problems in their imagination and will project them in ideological forms of consciousness. Thus ideology is a resolution in the mind of contradictions which are not practically resolved. The effect of a purely mental resolution is the concealment of the contradiction and its reproduction (see Larrain, 1979 and 1983). Hence, not all ideas, not even all the ideas of the ruling class, are necessarily ideological unless they explain away social contradictions. And yet all ideas are socially determined. But this does not necessarily involve bias, partiality or restricted validity.

Social determination must also be understood in the context of practice in so far as ideas are the expression − real or illusory − of human practices. Yet one should not reduce the social determination of ideas to an investigation of the originating social situation. Historical materialism does not seek to reduce the forms of social consciousness to their social background. The fact that the forms of social consciousness − works of literature and art or theoretical and scientific works − survive beyond their originating social conditions indicates that determination is both more subtle and more complicated a problem than it appears at first sight. Kosik has perceptively pointed out that a work's life is neither a mere result of the work itself nor a mere result of external circumstances: 'the work's life is not the result of its autonomous existence but of the *mutual interaction of the work and mankind*' (Kosik, 1976, p. 81). A work of art survives not because it contains within itself a universal validity but because it can be inserted in, articulated with, and assume meaning for the practice of new generations. If this is so, then historical materialism cannot understand determination as a single causative act. Determination is a permanent process of production and reproduction of ideas within new contexts and practices which give them a renewed sense. Determination has to do not only with the genesis of ideas but also with their ability to survive. This is why it should be understood as a continuous process whereby ideas are produced but also reanimated by new social practices.

It should be noted that this concept of determination goes beyond the traditional conception of the determination of ideas by the economic structure. This is not because I want to deny the determining effects of the economic structure but because a concept of determination based on the sole effectivity of the economic structure is problematic. As the sum total of production relations, the economic structure certainly sets limits to the production of ideas and to the character of political and educational institutions. But, if one reduces the concept of determination to the 'setting of limits' by a structural arrangement, one is bound to encounter one of two problems. Either the setting of limits is a mere condition which fixes a general framework within which many practical options are taken and many possible ideas can be developed, in which case one does not know why certain options are taken or certain ideas are developed instead of others equally compatible with the structural conditions, or the setting of limits is understood as a fully determining and sufficient cause which precisely brings about those practical activities and ideas required by the structure, in which case human beings have no option but to act in the specific direction and sense set by the structure.

It seems to me that the concept of determination can go further than the first option and yet not deny human freedom as the second option. This can be done by introducing the concept of practice. The economic structure is considered as a condition of social practices which sets limits and certain options, but it is only the social practices themselves that determine more specifically the ideas which human beings develop. Thus, for instance, there is no doubt that the economic structure conditions and sets limits to the practices and ideas of the working class. But whether or not the working class develops specific revolutionary ideas ultimately depends on the character of its economic and political practice, on the form of its organization and concrete class struggles in which is involved. The economic structure can only establish a general interest in a particular direction but cannot secure its practical implementation. Of course this concept of determination by practice is far less precise than the determination by the structure proposed by Cohen. But at least it has the advantage of permitting the concrete investigation of the character and specificity of class practices and struggles which provide the clue to explain the particular forms of consciousness developed by the class. Determination by the economic structure alone does not require any specific investigation about class practices: they are supposed to conform to the pattern set by the structure, and so are class ideas. In this conception the only possible research is concerned with finding out why the expected political and ideological effects of the economic structure do not always come about. But the objective is to show the exceptional or aberrant nature of these cases. As Cohen would put it, 'a theory of history is not answerable to abnormal occurrences' (1978, p. 156).

Now, we have seen that, in so far as determination is concerned, the traditional orthodox view recently refurbished by Cohen maintains the primacy of productive forces which are supposed to have an inherent tendency to develop and therefore select those relations of production that can secure their development. Althusser, Balibar and Magaline, on the contrary, argue in favour of the primacy of relations of production. In this version the forces of production are merely the 'pertinent effects' or 'materialisation' of relations of production. Whatever the merits of the arguments in favour of each position, it seems to me that this kind of discussion is inherently limited because it is concerned with deciding which structural factor is ultimately determining, but it does not consider the possibility that neither of these two structural factors has primacy. I described this alternative as another tension in Marx and Engels's thought: is social change in antagonistic modes of production to be explained in terms of class struggle or in terms of structural factors and structural contradictions between them? Although Cohen maintains the primacy of productive forces and Althusser and Balibar maintain the primacy of relations of production, both agree that class struggle is derivative and non-explanatory because it is determined and required by the structures.

Both positions do not take into account the practical subjects when they explain the basic mechanism of change. For Cohen productive forces do not include human beings or any other social elements; they are material and inherently tend to progress regardless of human will and social organization. True, Cohen does say that 'history is the development of human power' but he immediately adds that 'the course of its development is not subject to human will' (1978, p. 148). For Althusser and Balibar relations of production cannot be reduced to relations between human beings nor are classes the subjects of them but merely their supports. For both positions practical subjects divided into classes are conceived as mere supports or bearers. But they forget what is for me crucial, namely, that both productive forces and relations of production are social results produced by human practice; they are crystallizations of the practical process whereby human beings produce their material existence. As such they certainly condition human beings, but these human beings can also modify and change them. Marx and Engels expressed this quite clearly:

> each stage contains a material result, a sum of productive forces, a historically created relation to nature and of individuals to one another, which is handed down to each generation from its predecessor; a mass of productive forces, capital funds and circumstances, which on the one hand is indeed modified by the new generation, but on the other also prescribes for it its conditions of life and gives it a definite development, a special character. It shows that circumstances make men just as much as men make circumstances. (GI, p. 54)

And again:

> forces of production and social relations — two different sides of the development of the social individual . . . Nature builds no machines, no locomotives, railways, electric telegraphs, self-acting mules etc. These are products of human industry . . . They are *organs of the human brain*, *created by the human hand*; the power of knowledge, objectified. (G, p. 706)

> every productive force is an acquired force the product of former activity. The productive forces are therefore the result of practically applied human energy; but this energy is itself conditioned by the circumstances in which men find themselves, by the productive forces already acquired, by the social form which exists before they exist. (letter to P. V. Annenkov, 28 December 1846, MESC, p. 30)

It does not make sense to me to concede 'primacy' to a social result, be it productive forces or relations of production. Primacy can only be attached to human beings' practical production and transformation of their material life. Of course, this practice necessarily involves both relations of production and productive forces as *results* and *preconditions* of material reproduction. But change cannot be fully explained as a structural effect of these social results. Change is only conditioned by them but not fully preordained. It is human beings with their practical activity that bring about change within a set of limited options. It is true that human beings do not choose freely their productive forces and relations of production – they are handed down to them by the preceding generation – but this does not make them absolutely powerless to change them nor does it preclude various possibilities in attempting to change them.

The tensions in Marx and Engels's conception of social change must therefore be resolved in favour of practical political activity and class struggle – not an absolutely arbitrary and random class struggle, of course, but a class struggle conditioned by the economic structure and the level of productive forces. Yet this conditioning does not eliminate choices it only limits them. The principal contradiction of any antagonistic mode of production is that which generates class struggle, that is to say the contradiction between the direct producers and the owners of the conditions of production, between peasants and feudal lords, between labour and capital. It is the struggle between these opposite extremes which brings about social change of importance. True, Marx and Engels spoke of the contradiction between productive forces and relations of production as the main cause of social change. The problem is that one cannot properly speak of a contradiction between them because by definition the terms of a contradiction must be mutually inclusive, each pole must be defined in opposition to the other so that they cannot exist on their own. Relations of production and productive forces are heterogeneous terms not inherently opposed to one another because at the beginning of a mode of production the former are supposed to stimulate the development of the latter. Many authors are aware of this problem. Schaff, for instance, suggests that in this context Marx uses 'contradiction' in a different sense, to mean 'that the productive forces of society *are unable* to function within the existing relations of production; that an *incompatibility* has arisen' (Schaff, 1960, p. 246). But obviously, it is not very satisfactory to work with different definitions of the same concept. Others, such as Magaline (1975, p. 63), Echeverría (1978, p. 223), and Bettelheim (1974, p. 23), suggest that instead of contradiction one should speak of a relation of *correspondence* and *non-correspondence*. At any rate, whereas the basic contradiction of a mode of production is constitutive of its very existence from its inception, a relation of non-correspondence emerges late in the evolution of the mode of production. Hence the principal contradiction between the direct producers and the owners of the conditions of production determines the emergence of this 'non-correspondence' or 'incompatibility' and not vice versa.

I must acknowledge the fact that of all the tensions I have found in Marx and Engels the tension concerning the explanation of social change is probably the one in which, on balance, Marx and Engels's own thought more clearly favours one pole, namely, the primacy of productive forces. The weight of evidence in this sense is quite impressive, particularly if one takes a wider interpretation than Cohen's and includes within productive forces forms of social co-operation. But in spite of this the task of reconstructing historical materialism demands that new balances are struck which can make it a better theory even if it is necessary to alter Marx and Engels's thought. Cohen has precisely criticized Plamenatz 'because he is disposed to see in society only a collection of activities, not positions' and 'concentrates on what he calls "social life" and fails to distinguish it from the social structure in which it occurs' (Cohen, 1974, p. 92). I am not myself defending Plamenatz's position and I accept that one must distinguish social practices from structural relations. I even accept Cohen's view that structural definitions alone 'may be used to reveal the network of ties connecting society's members' (1974, p. 93). Yet I disagree with Cohen's attempt to explain social changes as a direct and ineluctable result of structural relations and automatically to derive human behaviour from structurally defined role expectations. Structural relations and role expectations certainly influence and condition behaviour and hence change, but not with inevitable necessity.

Fleischer (1973) and Wellmer (1971) have introduced a valuable distinction between what is *practically necessary* and what is *inevitably necessary*. The latter is a change or mode of behaviour which is bound to occur. But this kind of necessity is outside the boundaries of historical materialism. Socialism in this sense is for historical materialism only a practical necessity, that is to say, a mode of life which has to be constructed, a task set for human beings to accomplish in which they may fail. But, of course, without certain structural conditions, socialism is an illusion or a dream. The very idea of socialism only appears with the emergence of capitalism where the conditions for it to be constructed are created for the first time. Nevertheless, a structural necessary condition is not inescapably sufficient, and this is why one cannot simply deduce that because the structural conditions for socialism are present then socialism is bound to happen. It only may happen if human beings succeed in practically bringing it about. This is by no means a foregone conclusion. Lukács rightly reminds us that Lenin believed that for capitalism there was 'no situation from which there is no way out. Whatever position capitalism may find itself in there will always be some "purely economic" solutions available' (Lukács, 1971, p. 306).

If this is so, then it is very difficult to accept Marx's description of the evolution of societies as a process of natural history governed by independent laws which inexorably lead to communism. At the very least the transition to socialism cannot be conceived in this way. Contrary to what one may expect, Marx's mature political writings show an increased awareness about the uncertainties of such a process as compared with more deterministic theoretical statements of some early writings. While in 1844 Marx and Engels maintained that 'It is not a question of what this or that proletarian, or even the whole proletariat, at the moment *regards* as its aim. It is a question of *what the proletariat is*, and what, in accordance with this *being*, it will historically be compelled to do' (HF, p. 44), in 1870 on the occasion of the Franco-Prussian war and referring to the European working classes Marx affirms that:

> If they forsake their duty, if they remain passive, the present tremendous war will be but the harbinger of still deadlier international feuds, and lead in every nation to a renewed triumph over the workman by the lords of the sword, of the soil, and of capital. (Address of the General Council to the members of First International, FIA, p. 186)

The confident description of proletarian class-consciousness as a necessary development derived from the proletariat's being is replaced by the conception that the achievement of class-consciousness very much depends on attitudes and practices which cannot be guaranteed and which must be developed amid 'circumstances of extreme difficulty' (p. 185).

The question arises whether the rejection of unilinearism and its replacement by the theory of practice transforms the historical process into a wholly indeterminate and chaotic affair with no discernible rationality, thus leaving Marxism vacuous (Gellner, 1983 and 1984). I do not think so. Yet the point is to ascertain what rationality in history means. It cannot mean a preordained sense which is prior to human practice, unless one wants to go back to the classic philosophies which presented history as the realization of the Idea, Reason or Providence. As Kosik has put it:

> Reason is not laid down throughout history ahead of time, in order to be revealed as reason in the historical process, but rather it *forms itself* as reason in the course of history. According to the providential conception, reason *designs* history, and is itself gradually revealed in history's realization. By contrast, according to the materialist conception, only in history is reason first formed; history is not *reasonably preordained* but only *becomes* reasonable. (Kosik, 1976, p. 144)

The sense of history, therefore, is not independent of human beings practically constructing their lives. In realizing themselves as practical beings, men do not follow a necessary plan. So the sense of history must be given in the practical process whereby human beings realize themselves. And, just as this process of practical construction of their lives is not absolutely free but is conditioned by material circumstances and relations which human beings themselves have produced, so is reason in history neither wholly predetermined nor infinite in its potentialities.

In a letter to P. V. Annekov, Marx argues that 'because of the simple fact that every succeeding generation finds itself in possession of the productive forces acquired by the previous generation, and that they serve it as the raw material for new production, a coherence arises in human history' (letter 28 December 1846, MESC, pp. 30–1). This means that there is a continuity in the way in which human beings make history, they do not have to start afresh every time from scratch. But it would be a mistake to believe that the sense of history is given in the accumulated material circumstances independently of human practices. Objectified forms of practice, productive forces and given relations of production are crucial for the emergence of a coherence in history but only in so far as they are connected with human practice because although they condition practice they are also transformed by practice. Ultimately it is human practice that gives conditions a sense. Therefore, the sense of history is constructed, is produced by the practical and conditioned deployment of human beings. This conception precludes the idea of a final goal which is bound to be achieved and rejects the conception of an immanent drive which leads history towards a necessary end. As Fleischer has put it:

> history is not progress to higher humanity and freedom, but merely the increased possibility of such progress. The inherent contingency of all history lies in the fact that the realization of the possible is always a matter of free initiatives and creative syntheses, the quality and success of which are not guaranteed in advance. (Fleischer, 1973, p. 80)

It is in this context that one can understand why Marx's ambivalence in respect of the results of colonialism in Asia and Ireland cannot be resolved once and for all in either of the two directions mentioned at the end of Chapter 1. The choice appeared to be between imperialism promoting the development of productive forces or being an obstacle to the industrialization of Third World countries. The latter has been the orthodox position since 1928, whereas recently Warren (1980) has tried to revive the former. Neither of these two extremes on its own fits a reconstructed historical materialism because they propose a fixed and ineluctable course of history which seems to be preordained prior to any concrete analysis. As I pointed out in Chapter 3, the experience of Third World countries after the Second World War has shown that although imperialism has not resulted in the full industrialization of satellite countries neither has it absolutely prevented the development of their productive forces. It is a travesty to maintain, as Warren does, that imperialism has been everywhere beneficial, but on the other hand it is impossible to deny the existence of somewhat dynamic processes of *dependent* development in some Third World countries. These two possibilities can coexist side by side because imperialism cannot be understood as a purely external imposition which produces similar results everywhere, but, as Cardoso and Faletto (1979) have argued, imperialism is always mediated by, and exercises its influence in articulation with, the internal class struggle of the Third World countries.

MAIN TENETS OF RECONSTRUCTED HISTORICAL MATERIALISM

At the end of this work it is perhaps useful to identify more schematically the most important principles which a reconstructed historical materialism propounds and the specific perspective it contributes to social sciences. In order to do this I shall consider four interrelated areas or points of view: society consciousness, history and the individual.

Society
1   Society is not a simple sum of individuals 'but expresses the sum of interrelations, the relations within which these individuals stand' (G, p. 265). But this conception must be complemented with the idea that society, whatever its form

is 'the product of men's reciprocal action' (letter to P. V. Annenkov, 28 December 1846, MESC, p. 30). Human beings enter into social relations in the process of practically producing their lives.

2   Therefore, in order to understand society it is necessary to look first of all at the process of production, the process whereby individuals transform nature which is simultaneously a co-operative or social process.

3   Neither society nor production should be analysed 'in general' but must be considered in 'historical form'.

4   The concept of 'mode of production' provides the clue to the historical analysis of society and involves the combination of a specific system of production relations with a certain level of productive forces.

5   The system of relations of production includes both a specific form of control over the means of production and a specific form of extraction of surplus labour. It therefore determines a specific class distinction between the direct producers and those who control the means of production, and a legal and political system which secures both the property of the means of production and the extraction of surplus labour.

6   Historical materialism starts with the analysis of the capitalist mode of production from which it can develop the necessary concepts and insights to analyse other modes of production.

7   The concept of mode of production is an abstract analytical tool which permits the analysis of concrete social formations. Hence a mode of production is not a 'historical stage' nor can one derive from its internal logic the concrete evolution and expected development of a particular society. Most concrete societies or social formations possess more than one mode of production.

8 In any particular society the relations of production and productive forces determined by the specific combination of modes of production in existence constitute the basic set of circumstances which conditions individuals and their practice. But individuals can try to transform those circumstances within a finite set of options which the very circumstances allow. Social change is therefore neither arbitrary nor absolutely predetermined.

Consciousness
1 Social consciousness is produced in the context of social practices and it is not a mere reflection of a seemingly objective reality but anticipates the results of practice.

2 In so far as the ruling class is the ruling material force of society 'the ideas of the ruling class are in every epoch the ruling ideas' (GI, p. 59).

3 Historical materialism identifies a specific form of distorted consciousness which conceals contradiction and is called *ideology*. Ideology should not be confused with ruling ideas. Not all ruling ideas necessarily mask contradictions.

4 Although all ideology serves the interests of the ruling class, because by concealing contradictions it helps to reproduce them, it is not only the ruling class that produces ideology. All classes including the proletariat can produce ideology because they are involved in a 'limited material mode of activity'.

5 All ideas are socially determined but not all ideas are ideological.

6 The social determination of consciousness is a continuous process of revitalization of intellectual and artistic works in the context of new practices. The validity of ideas is not confined to the social setting from which they originated.

7 Science differs from common sense in seeking to penetrate

the appearances of reality in order to reach the inner relations. This entails the construction of concepts and models which have no direct empirical referent.

8   The method of historical materialism does not lay claim to any special 'dialectical logic' and can be said to be dialectical only in so far as its object of study is dialectical. A dialectical reality which moves in a contradictory form can and must be studied according to the rules of formal logic.

History

1   There is no inherent overall meaning of or necessary end to history. 'History is nothing but the activity of men in pursuit of their ends' (HF, p. 110). History is not the realization of a preordained plan.

2   History 'becomes' rational in the process whereby human beings practically deploy themselves. So it is the practical activity of human beings that gives history its meaning. There is no pre-established rationality of history.

3   Historical materialism is a non-teleological theory. It does not propound a final goal which is bound to come nor does it believe in a natural and immanent drive which propels history forward.

4   Historical materialism rejects a unilinear conception which sketches 'the general path of development prescribed by fate to all nations' (MESC, p. 293)

5   Human beings individuate themselves through the process of history but history cannot be deduced from human nature or human essence.

6   Progress in technology and in the quality of social relations is not inherent in history but it is a possibility which depends on human practice when the right social conditions are given.

7   Although contradictions have been the basis of historical

change for most of our civilized history, historical materialism does not maintain that all historical change is caused by contradiction and class struggle. This has been the case only for societies in which antagonistic modes of production predominate and only in respect of major social changes.

8   History is made by human beings even if they do not realize that they make it and even if they do not control its results. However, historical materialism puts forward the idea that it is now possible for human beings consciously to make history by overcoming all forms of class domination and collectively controlling their social relations.

The Individual
1   Although historical materialism is not primarily a theory about individuality, many consequences for the conception of the individual derive from it. For a start, historical materialism emphasizes the active side of individuals. By means of practice human beings not only reproduce their material life and the society they live in but also, by 'acting on the external world and changing it', they at the same time change 'their own nature' (K, Vol. 1, p. 173)

2   But human beings do not act entirely according to their free will, they are conditioned by the objectified products of their own practice: they are born into certain social relations they have not chosen and receive certain productive forces from the past.

3   Although circumstances condition human beings, human beings can change circumstances and this is conceived as revolutionary practice.

4   Human beings can individuate themselves only in the midst of society (G, p. 84) and through the process of history (G, p. 496)

5   Historical materialism finds in history a process of individuation which has taken place within ever more

developed and complex social relations. At the beginning, the individual almost does not count, human beings are totally dependent on a greater whole as part of the clan and herd first, and personally dependent upon a master or landlord later. With capitalism individuals acquire personal independence which is nevertheless 'founded on objective dependence', that is to say, 'social relations which have become independent and now enter into opposition to the seemingly independent individuals . . . in such a way that individuals are now ruled by *abstractions*, whereas earlier they depended on one another' (G, p. 164).

6 Historical materialism proposes the idea that a third stage is possible in this process of individuation: 'free individuality, based on the universal development of individuals and on their subordination of their communal, social productivity as their social wealth' (G, p. 158). However, although the second capitalist stage creates the conditions for the third, this is not an automatic process but a task set for human practice to accomplish, a task in which individuals may fail.

7 Historical materialism does not propose a future collectivism which dissolves the individual in the community but rather a society where the free development of each individual is the condition for the free development of all.

8 Historical materialism does not propose a 'class humanism' as opposed to personal freedom (Althusser). Historical materialism conceives of class as assuming 'an independent existence as against the individuals, so that the latter find their conditions of life predetermined . . . thus becoming subsumed under it' (GI, p. 77), and hence it seeks the liberation of individuals by the abolition of all classes, including the proletariat.

References

ABBREVIATIONS OF MARX'S AND ENGELS'S WORKS

AD   Engels, F., *Anti-Dühring* (London: Lawrence & Wishart, 1975).

AOIC   Marx, K., 'Articles on India and China', in SFE.

BRUM   Marx, K., *The Eighteenth Brumaire of Louis Bonaparte*, in MESW.

CCPE   Marx, K., *A Contribution to the Critique of Political Economy* (Moscow: Progress, 1977).

CHDS   Marx, K., *Critique of Hegel's Doctrine of the State*, in EW.

CM   Marx, K., and Engels, F., *Manifesto of the Communist Party*, in MESW.

DB   Engels, F., 'Die Bewegungen von 1847', *Deutsche Brüsseler Zeitung*, 23 January 1848, in MHAL.

DON   Engels, F., *Dialectics of Nature* (Moscow: Progress, 1974).

EPM   Marx, K., *Economic and Philosophical Manuscripts*, in EW.

EW   Marx, K., *Early Writings* (Harmondsworth: Penguin, 1975).

FIA   Marx, K., *The First International and After* (Harmondsworth: Penguin, 1974).

G   Marx, K., *Grundrisse* (Harmondsworth: Penguin, 1973).

GI   Marx, K., and Engels, F., *The German Ideology, Collected Works*, Vol. 5 (London: Lawrence & Wishart, 1976).

HF   Marx, K., and Engels, F., *The Holy Family* (Moscow: Progress, 1975).

K   Marx, K., *Capital*, Vols 1, 2 and 3 (London: Lawrence & Wishart, 1974).

LF   Engels, F., *Ludwig Feuerbach and the End of Classical German Philosophy*, in MESW.

LOI   Marx, K., 'Letters on Ireland', in FIA.

MESC   Marx, K., and Engels, F., *Selected Correspondence* (Moscow: Progress, 1975).

MESW   Marx, K., and Engels, F., *Selected Works in One Volume* (London: Lawrence & Wishart, 1970).

MHAL   Marx, K., and Engels, F., *Materiales para la historia de América Latina* (Mexico: Cuadernos de Pasado y Presente, 1980).

OFPS   Engels, F., *The Origin of the Family, Private Property and the State*, in MESW.

PP   Marx, K., *The Poverty of Philosophy* (Moscow: Progress, 1975).

PWG   Engels, F., *The Peasant War in Germany* (London: Lawrence & Wishart, 1969).

REV   Marx, K., *The Revolutions of 1848* (Harmondsworth: Penguin, 1973).

RKM   Engels, F., Review of Karl Marx's *A Contribution to the Critique of Political Economy*, *Das Volk*, nos 14 and 16 (1859), in CCPE.

SFE   Marx, K., *Surveys from Exile* (Harmondsworth: Penguin, 1973).

SUS   Engels, F., *Socialism: Utopian and Scientific*, in MESW.

TOF   Marx, K., 'Theses on Feuerbach', in GI.

TSV   Marx, K., *Theories of Surplus-Value*, Vols 1, 2 and 3 (London: Lawrence & Wishart, 1969).

WPP   Marx, K., *Wages, Price and Profit*, in MESW.

OTHER AUTHORS CITED

Acton, H. B. (1955), *The Illusion of the Epoch* (London: Cohen & West).

Adler, A. (1983), *Theses, Resolutions and Manifestos of the First Four Congresses of the Third International* (London: Pluto Press).

Agosti, A. (1976), *La Terza Internazionale, storia documentaria*, Vol. 2, 1924–28 (Roma: Editori Riuniti).

Althusser, L. (1971), *Lenin and Philosophy and Other Essays* (London: New Left Books).

Althusser, L. (1976), *Essays in Self-Criticism* (London: New Left Books).

Althusser, L., and Balibar, E. (1975), *Reading Capital* (London: New Left Books).

Anderson, P. (1978), *Passages from Antiquity to Feudalism* (London: Verso).

Anderson, P. (1979a), *Considerations on Western Marxism* (London: Verso).

Anderson, P. (1979b), *Lineages of the Absolutist State* (London: Verso).

Anderson, P. (1980), *Arguments within English Marxism* (London: Verso).

Anderson, P. (1983), *In the Tracks of Historical Materialism* (London: Verso).

Baran, P. A. (1957), *The Political Economy of Growth* (New York: Monthly Review Press).

Bertrand, M. (1979), *Le Marxisme et l'histoire* (Paris: Éditions Sociales).

Bettelheim, C. (1974), *La Transition vers l'économie socialiste* (Paris: Maspéro).

Bhaskar, R. (1983), 'Dialectics', in *A dictionary of Marxist Thought*, ed. T. B. Bottomore (Oxford: Blackwell).

Bober, M. M. (1968), *Karl Marx's Interpretation of History* (Cambridge, Mass.: Harvard University Press).

Bogulavsky, B. M., *et al.* (1978), *ABC of Dialectical and Historical Materialism* (Moscow: Progress).

Bottomore, T. B. (1964), *Elites and Society* (Harmondsworth: Penguin).

Bukharin, N. (1965), *Historical Materialism, a System of Sociology* (New York: Russell & Russell).

Cardoso, F. H., and Faletto, E. (1979), *Dependency and Development in Latin America* (Berkeley Calif.: University of California Press).

Carver, T. (1983), *Marx and Engels: the Intellectual Relationship* (Brighton: Wheatsheaf Books).

Cohen, G. A. (1970), 'On some criticisms of historical materialism', *Proceedings of the Aristotelian Society*, supplement, vol. 44.

Cohen, G. A. (1974), 'Being, consciousness and roles: on the foundations of historical materialism', in *Essays in Honour of E. H. Carr*, ed. C. Abramsky (London: Macmillan).

Cohen, G. A. (1978), *Karl Marx's Theory of History, a Defence* (Oxford: Clarendon Press).

Cohen, G. A. (1983a), 'Forces and relations of production', in *Marx: A Hundred Years on*, ed. B. Matthews (London: Lawrence & Wishart).

Cohen, G. A. (1983b), 'Reconsidering historical materialism', in *Marxism*, ed. J. R. Pennock and J. W. Chapman, *Nomos*, no. 26.

Cohen, J. (1982), Review of *Karl Marx's Theory of History: a Defence*, *The Journal of Philosophy*, vol. 79, no. 5.

Colletti, L. (1975), 'Marxism and the dialectic', *New Left Review* no. 93.

Cornforth, M. (1977), *Dialectical materialism*, Vol. 2: *Historical Materialism* (London: Lawrence & Wishart).

Cotten, J. P. (1977), 'Peut-on "isoler" la dialectique (lois, catégories et pratiques sociales)?', in *Sur la dialectique*, ed. Centre d'Études et de Recherches Marxistes (Paris: Éditions Sociales).

Echeverría, R. (1978), 'Marx's concept of science', D.Phil. thesis, University of London.

Federn, K. (1939), *The Materialist Conception of History* (London: Macmillan).

Fleischer, H. (1973), *Marxism and History* (London: Allen Lane).

Frank, A. G. (1969), *Capitalism and Underdevelopment in Latin America* (New York: Monthly Review Press).

Gellner, E. (1983), 'Stagnation without salvation', *Times Literary Supplement*, 14 January.

Gellner, E. (1984), 'Along the historical highway', *Times Literary Supplement*, 16 March.

Gerratana, V. (1975), *Investigaciones sobre la historia del Marxismo*, Vols 1 and 2 (Barcelona: Grijalbo).

Giddens, A. (1981), *A Contemporary Critique of Historical Materialism* (London: Macmillan).

Godelier, M. (1972), *Rationality and Irrationality in Economics* (London: Macmillan).

Habermas, J. (1972), *Knowledge and Human Interests* (London: Heinemann).

Habermas, J. (1979), *Communication and the Evolution of Society* (London: Heinemann).

Habermas, J. (1982), 'A reply to my critics', in *Habermas, Critical Debates*, ed. J. B. Thompson and D. Held (London: Macmillan).

Harnecker, M. (1968), *Los conceptos elementales del materialismo histórico* (Mexico: Siglo Veintiuno).

Hegel, G. W. F. (1975), *Logic* (Oxford: Clarendon Press).

Hegel, G. W. F. (1976), *The Science of Logic* (London: Allen & Unwin).

Hegel, G. W. F. (1977), *The Phenomenology of Mind* (London: Allen & Unwin).

Heilbroner, R. L. (1980), *Marxism: For and Against* (New York: W. W. Norton).

Hellèr, A. (1982), 'Habermas and Marxism', in *Habermas, Critical Debates*, ed. J. B. Thompson and D. Held (London: Macmillan).

Herf, J. (1977), 'Science and class or philosophy and revolution: Perry Anderson on Western Marxism', *Socialist Revolution*, no. 35, vol. 7, no. 5.

Hindess, B., and Hirst, P. Q. (1975), *Pre-Capitalist Modes of Production* (London: Routledge & Kegan Paul).

Hoffman, J. (1975), *Marxism and the Theory of Practice* (London: Lawrence & Wishart).

Hook, S. (1955), *Marx and the Marxists, the Ambiguous Legacy* (Princeton NJ: Van Nostrand).

Jaeglé, P. (1977), 'Dialectique de la nature: sur quelques concepts (qualité, quantité . . .), in *Sur la dialectique*, ed. Centre d'Études et de Recherches Marxistes (Paris: Éditions Sociales).

Kautsky, K. (1927), *Die Materialistische Geschichtsauffassung* (Berlin: J. H. W. Dietz).

Kautsky, K. (1975a), *Etica y concepción materialista de la historia* (Cordoba: Cuadernos de Pasado y Presente).

Kautsky, K. (1975b), *La doctrina socialista, Bernstein y la social-democracia alemana* (Barcelona: Fontanamara).

Kelle, V., and Kovalson, M. (1973), *Historical Materialism, an Outline of Marxist Theory of Society* (Moscow: Progress).

Kolakowski, L. (1978), *Main Currents of Marxism*, Vols 1, 2 and 3 (Oxford: Clarendon Press).

Korsch, K. (1938), *Karl Marx* (London: Chapman & Hall).

Korsch, K. (1973), *L'Anti-Kautsky* (Paris: Éditions Champ Libre).

Kosik, K. (1976), *Dialectics of the Concrete* (Dordrecht: D. Reidel).

Kuusinen, O., *et al.* (1963), *Fundamentals of Marxism-Leninism* (Moscow: Foreign Languages Publishing House).

Labriola, A. (1970), *Essais sur la conception matérialiste de l'histoire* (Paris: Gordon & Breach).

Laclau, E. (1969), 'Modos de producción, sistemas económicos y población excedente, aproximación histórica a los casos argentino y chileno', *Revista Latinoamericana de Sociología*, vol. 5, no. 2.

Laclau, E. (1977), *Politics and Ideology in Marxist Theory* (London: New Left Books).

Lange, O. (1974), *Political Economy*, Vol. 1 (Oxford: Pergamon Press).

Larrain, J. (1979), *The Concept of Ideology* (London: Hutchinson).

Larrain, J. (1983), *Marxism and Ideology* (London: Macmillan).

Leff, G. (1961), *The Tyranny of Concepts: a Critique of Marxism* (London: Merlin Press).

Lenin, V. I. (1972a) [1909], *Materialism and Empirio-Criticism* (Peking: Foreign Languages Press).

Lenin, V. I. (1972b) [1933], *Philosophical Notebooks*, in *Collected Works*, Vol. 38 (London: Lawrence & Wishart).

Lenin, V. I. (1974) [1899], *The Development of Capitalism in Russia* (Moscow: Progress).

Lenin, V. I. (1975) [1917], *Imperialism, the Highest Stage of Capitalism* (Peking: Foreign Languages Press).

Lenin, V. I. (1976) [1894], 'What the 'friends of the people' are and how they fight the social-democrats', in *On Historical Materialism*, K. Marx *et al.* (Moscow: Progress).

Levine, A., and Wright, E. O. (1980), 'Rationality and class struggle', *New Left Review*, no. 123.

Lobkowics, N. (1967), *Theory and Practice: History of the Concept from Aristotle to Marx* (Notre Dame, Ind.: University of Notre Dame Press).

Lukács, G. (1971), *History and Class Consciousness* (London: Merlin Press).

Luxemburg, R. (1951), *The Accumulation of Capital* (London: Routledge & Kegan Paul).

Magaline, A. D. (1975), *Lutte de classes et dévalorisation du capital* (Paris: Maspéro).

Mannheim, K. (1972), *Ideology and Utopia* (London: Routledge & Kegan Paul).

Márkus, G. (1983), 'Concepts of ideology in Marx', *Canadian Journal of political and social theory*, vol. 7, no. 1–2.

McLennan, G. (1981), *Marxism and the Methodologies of History* (London: Verso and New Left Books).

McMurtry, J. (1978), *The Structure of Marx's World-View* (Princeton, NJ: Princeton University Press).

Melotti, U. (1982), *Marx and the Third World* (London: Macmillan).

Miller, R. W. (1981), 'Productive forces and the forces of change: a review of Gerald A. Cohen, *Karl Marx's Theory of History: a Defence*', *The Philosophical Review*, vol. 90, no. 1.

Palma, G. (1978), 'Dependency: a formal theory of underdevelopment or a methodology for the analysis of concrete situations of underdevelopment', *World Development*, vol. 6, no. 7–8.

Plamenatz, J. (1971). *Ideology* (London: Macmillan).

Plekhanov, G. (1972), *The Development of the Monist View of History* (Moscow: Progress).

Plekhanov, G. (1976a), *The Materialist Conception of History* (London: Lawrence & Wishart).

Plekhanov, G. (1976b), *The Role of the Individual in History* (London: Lawrence & Wishart).

Plekhanov, G. (n.d.a), *Fundamental Problems of Marxism* (London: Lawrence & Wishart).

Plekhanov, G. (n.d.b), Preface to the German edition of F. Engels's *Ludwig Feuerbach and the End of Classical German Philosophy*, appendix in *Fundamental Problems of Marxism* (London: Lawrence & Wishart).

Pompa, L. (1982), 'Defending Marx's theory of history', *Inquiry*, no. 23.

Popper, K. (1973), *The Open Society and its Enemies*, Vols 1 and 2 (London: Routledge & Kegan Paul).

Popper, K. (1976), *Conjectures and Refutations* (London: Routledge & Kegan Paul).

Poster, M. (1979), *Sartre's Marxism* (London: Pluto Press).

Poulantzas, N. (1977), *Fascism and Dictatorship* (London: New Left Books).

Poulantzas, N. (1978), *L'État, le pouvoir, le socialisme* (Paris: Presses Universitaires de France).

Rey, P. P. (1978), *Les Alliances de classes* (Paris: Maspéro).

Salvadori, M. (1979), *Karl Kautsky and the Socialist Revolution 1880–1938* (London: New Left Books).

Sartre, J. P. (1968), *Search for a Method* (New York: Vintage Books).

Sartre, J. P. (1976), *Critique of Dialectical Reason* (London: New Left Books).

Schaff, A. (1960), 'Marxist dialectics and the principle of contradiction', *Journal of Philosophy*, vol. 57, no. 7.

Schmidt, A. (1971), *The Concept of Nature in Marx* (London: New Left Books).

Sereni, E. (1971), 'De Marx à Lénine: la categorie de "formation économique et sociale" ', *La Pensée*, no. 159.

Sève, L. (1974), 'Pré-rapport sur la dialectique', in *Lénine et la pratique scientifique*, ed. Centre d'Études et de Recherches Marxistes (Paris: Éditions Sociales).

Shaw, W. H. (1978), *Marx's Theory of History* (London: Hutchinson).

Stalin, J. V. (1976), *Dialectical and Historical Materialism*, in *Problems of Leninism*, (Peking: Foreign Languages Press).

Ste Croix, G. E. M. de (1983), *The Class Struggle in the Ancient Greek World* (London: Duckworth).

Ste Croix, G. E. M. de (1984), 'Class in Marx's conception of history, ancient and modern', *New Left Review*, no. 146.

Sutcliffe, B. (1972), 'Imperialism and industrialization in the Third

World', in *Studies in the Theory of Imperialism*, ed. R. Owen and B. Sutcliffe (London: Longman).

Texier, J. (1971), 'Désaccords sur la définition des concepts', *La Pensée*, no. 159.

Thompson, E. P. (1978), *The Poverty of Theory and Other Essays* (London: Merlin Press).

Warren, B. (1980), *Imperialism Pioneer of Capitalism*, (London: Verso).

Wellmer, A. (1971), *Critical Theory of Society* (New York: Herder & Herder).

Willer, D., and Willer, J. (1973), *Systematic Empiricism: a Critique of a Pseudoscience* (Englewood Cliffs, NJ: Prentice-Hall).

Williams, R. (1977), *Marxism and Literature* (Oxford: Oxford University Press).

Wright, E. O. (1983), 'Giddens's critique of Marxism', *New Left Review*, no. 138.

Index